Globalisation of industrial activities

Four Case Studies:

Auto Parts, Chemicals, Construction and Semiconductors

ORGANISATION FOR ECONOMIC CO-OPERATION AND DEVELOPMENT

ORGANISATION FOR ECONOMIC CO-OPERATION AND DEVELOPMENT

Pursuant to Article 1 of the Convention signed in Paris on 14th December 1960, and which came into force on 30th September 1961, the Organisation for Economic Co-operation and Development (OECD) shall promote policies designed:

— to achieve the highest sustainable economic growth and employment and a rising standard of living in Member countries, while maintaining financial stability, and thus to contribute to the development of the world economy;

— to contribute to sound economic expansion in Member as well as non-member countries in the process of economic development; and

— to contribute to the expansion of world trade on a multilateral, non-discriminatory basis in accordance with international obligations.

The original Member countries of the OECD are Austria, Belgium, Canada, Denmark, France, Germany, Greece, Iceland, Ireland, Italy, Luxembourg, the Netherlands, Norway, Portugal, Spain, Sweden, Switzerland, Turkey, the United Kingdom and the United States. The following countries became Members subsequently through accession at the dates indicated hereafter: Japan (28th April 1964), Finland (28th January 1969), Australia (7th June 1971) and New Zealand (29th May 1973). The Commission of the European Communities takes part in the work of the OECD (Article 13 of the OECD Convention). Yugoslavia has a special status at OECD (agreement of 28th October 1961).

Publié en français sous le titre :
LA MONDIALISATION INDUSTRIELLE
Quatre études de cas : Pièces automobiles,
produits chimiques, construction et semi-conducteurs

FOREWORD

The globalisation of industrial activities has prompted new questions about the efficacy of national industrial and trade policies and their linkages. Largely due to the internationalisation of firms, industrial policies are having greater impacts on trade in goods and services and trade policies have enlarged implications for industrial development. Such overlaps coupled with the phenomenon of industrial globalisation call for increased monitoring of the effects of OECD industrial policies as well as new multilateral approaches to policy formulation.

This report examines current issues in industrial trade in case studies of the automotive parts, chemicals, international construction and semiconductor industries. The case studies are preceded by a general overview and synthesis of the industrial policy issues emerging from the globalisation of industrial activities. It is based on work undertaken in the framework of the activities of the Industry Committee devoted to the globalisation of industry and was prepared by Candice Stevens of the Secretariat with the help of external consultants. In November 1990, the Industry Committee recommended the derestriction of this report, which is published under the responsibility of the Secretary-General.

ALSO AVAILABLE

TABLE OF CONTENTS

SUMMARY AND MAJOR ISSUES

CASE OF STUDIES

THE AUTOMOTIVE PARTS INDUSTRY

THE CHEMICALS INDUSTRY

THE INTERNATIONAL CONSTRUCTION INDUSTRY

THE SEMICONDUCTOR INDUSTRY

SUMMARY AND MAJOR ISSUES

I. INTERNATIONALISATION OF INDUSTRIAL ACTIVITIES

A. Changing Patterns of Competition

The internationalisation of OECD industry has proceeded in three broad stages with profound effects on the nature of global competition. In the post-war era, international trade was the main catalyst of economic growth.

Trade between nations expanded rapidly as tariffs and quotas were reduced through multilateral agreements. This period, extending through the late 1960s, has been called the golden age of trade. In this era, the degree of internationalisation of a country and its enterprises was measured primarily in terms of export shares and import penetration.

The next phase of internationalisation was marked by its emphasis on foreign investment. Evident in the 1950s and 1960s, investment in foreign production facilities became an even more popular mechanism of industrial expansion in the 1970s. Shifts in patterns of international economic activity and competition between multinational corporations were the main issues of the day. The measures used to assess the extent of internationalisation of a country and its companies came to include the proportion of global sales accounted for by production abroad.

In the 1980s, a third phase of internationalisation emerged largely due to the influence of technology. The ability to innovate and to adapt and implement technologies became key to industrial competitiveness; related advantages were found in new patterns of intangible investment and industrial organisation. To compete globally, companies increasingly needed technological sophistication, maximum flexibility, customised products and extensive supplier networks. The factories of the Ford era, mass production of standardised products, strict divisions of labour and single-site manufacturing were no longer adequate. International competition came to be governed in part by microelectronics and information technology.

This third phase of internationalisation is characterised by new patterns of industrial linkages. Corporations now interact on a global scale through a wide range of external alliances – e.g., joint ventures, subcontracting, licensing and interfirm agreements. Firms have gone beyond their traditional practices of exporting to foreign countries and building foreign facilities to establishing intricate international networks of research, production and information. These flexible webs of interaction exist alongside trade and foreign investment as evidence of the increasing globalisation of industrial activities, but have proven far more difficult to measure. For the most part, the trends indicated by the data in this study have continued to the present time.

The current phase of internationalisation has also brought a change in the notion of the comparative advantage of nations. The traditional paradigm based a country's comparative advantage on collective factors such as natural resources, labour and capital inputs. Today, the world's corporations look to all nations to gain advantages in production, marketing and research, in effect reducing the comparative advantage of a country to its contribution to their global strategies. Most corporate decisions are taken within a global frame of reference and are based on diverse relationships between multinational firms. But while companies often cooperate with their competitors to gain technology advantages, particularly in the intermediate components stage, they still compete keenly in final markets.

The internationalisation of industrial activities has been accompanied by an upheaval in international economic relations and growing trade and investment frictions. Large trade imbalances have emerged in the OECD area. Many OECD countries – in North America, Europe and Asia-Pacific – are initiating or reinforcing regional groupings to obtain advantages in industrial production and trade. At the same time, the newly industrialised economies (NIEs) have become competitive producers of manufactured products and account for over 10 per cent of world exports. Many developing countries as well as the East European countries are seeking fuller integration into global industrial networks. Governments are trying to reorient industrial and trade policies and to adapt national and international economic rules to cope with the changing patterns of global competition.

B.   Trends in Internationalisation

Trends in the internationalisation of industrial activities are not uniform but tend to vary by industrial sector (see Table 1). Companies in some industries (particularly some service sectors) have not internationalised to a great extent but remain largely domestic activities. There are sectors at the early stages of internationalisation which primarily engage in trade, while others have advanced to more sophisticated forms of globalisation such as technology alliances. Some sectors have firms which engage in several forms of internationalisation, while others prefer one type such as licensing or disdain a particular avenue such as foreign investment. Traditionally in most industries, a limited number of large multinationals dominated foreign activity while smaller firms stayed at home. Internationalisation in its most advanced forms remains an OECD-led process, dominated by firms from the major OECD countries (and more recently the NIEs); many other countries are not really involved.

International trade is still the most widespread form of the internationalisation of industrial activities. Despite the increase in other types of internationalisation (e.g., foreign investment, interfirm agreements), the growth in world commerce continues to be rapid. World merchandise exports expanded at an average annual rate of about 6 per cent between 1950 and 1988 (compared to 4.5 per cent growth in world output) and an estimated 7 per cent in 1989. Omitted from these figures is the increasing trade in services. Overall, the value of world trade including services is now approaching US$4 000 billion a year. Growth in trade of resource- and labour-intensive commodities has been relatively slower than that of technology-based and differentiated products. Goods and services trade is also changing in character as intra-firm trade and intra-industry trade (trade between countries in similar products) account for a larger portion. Intra-industry trade jumped dramatically in the 1980s after remaining constant in the 1970s. These newer types of trade, which are prompted by specialised consumer demands, technological factors and the benefits of international sourcing, reflect the new dynamics of global competition.

Foreign investment is a popular avenue for the internationalisation of industrial activities. Most outward-oriented firms progress from export-led expansion to establishing international production or assembly facilities. Foreign investment has long been extensive in some sectors (e.g., chemicals, food products) which derive advantages from market proximity; is growing in

12

Table 1. **Trends in Internationalisation**

Form	Purpose	Sector Examples
International Trade	To expand markets and increase returns to investment	Many sectors
Foreign Investment	To increase access to markets and localise production	Food Products Chemicals Automobiles
International Subcontracting	To allow specialisation in core components and increase flexibility	Aerospace Construction Automobiles
International Licensing	To broaden markets and increase returns from R&D expenditures	Pharmaceuticals Semiconductors
Cross-Border Mergers and Acquisitions	To increase scale economies and localise production	Electronics Financial Services
International Joint Ventures	To increase market access and pool resources	Minerals Machine Tools
International Interfirm Agreements	To share costs and risks of internationalisation	Aerospace Electronics

others (e.g., automobiles); and is negligible in those which have high fixed costs and scale economies and where market proximity is less important (e.g., aerospace, steel). The unique aspect of the current wave of international investment is geographical. In the 1950s and 1960s, it was globally-oriented American companies that established foreign production facilities, primarily in Europe. In the 1980s, it was globally-oriented Japanese and European companies that supported their export strategies through foreign investment. The United States is now the most important destination for investment flows; in 1982-89, more foreign direct investment went to the United States than to all other OECD countries combined. At present, Japanese companies are investing abroad (in automobiles, chemicals and electrical machinery) at roughly twice the rate of US companies and three times that of German companies. Intra-European investment is increasing in anticipation of the completion of the European single market at yearend 1992 and foreign investment in Japan is slowly growing from its present relatively low level.

Subcontracting is a form of internationalisation which may eventually lead to some downturn in foreign investment. Technological developments have facilitated the spinning off of production tasks to foreign firms which possess cost, technical or locational advantages. On an international basis, complex subcontracting arrangements centered around a prime contractor are found in sectors as diverse as aerospace and construction. Subcontracting is now spreading to other sectors, such as automobiles, where car makers wish to concentrate on the design and production of core components leaving peripherals to subcontractors. In several sectors, multinational companies are evolving into specialised designers and assemblers of components made by subcontractors from different parts of the world.

International **licensing** has been an important alternative to foreign investment in sectors such as pharmaceuticals where R&D investments are protected by patents. Here, firms may sell access to technology or know-how in exchange for a fee or royalties. Common in mature sectors where technology is embodied in a finished product, patent licensing is used to gain access to distribution networks in foreign countries and to increase returns to research. Licensing is not an international strategy in sectors with strong links between research and marketing, such as automobiles or telecommunications. International cross-licensing is a more sophisticated form of licensing popular in sectors such as semiconductors, which use this two-way exchange of technology to reduce R&D costs.

Cross-border **mergers and acquisitions** are gaining in popularity as a means to create economies of scale in research, production and marketing as well as to localise production. The current trend to international mergers and acquisitions is part of the strategy to serve foreign markets from local production rather than exports. While these transactions have involved a wide range of industries, they have recently been concentrated in computers, telecommunications and consumer electronics. Other busy sectors for mergers and acquisitions are food and food retailing, insurance and banking and finance. Previously a cross-Atlantic phenomenon between American and European firms, international acquisitions have become an important Japanese enterprise strategy. Japanese firms surpassed British companies in US takeovers for the first time in 1989. However, there was also a powerful increase in European activity by US companies in 1989 when they accounted for over 30 per cent of all cross-border acquisitions in western Europe.

There are signs that international **joint ventures,** a traditional instrument for entering markets, will be a popular choice for multinational firms in the 1990s. Equity holdings in a venture are divided among partners who share the costs and risks of technology development, production or marketing. Joint ventures allow more rapid market access than exports and have lower costs than foreign investment. However, the legal contract which binds firms with different cultural, economic and political backgrounds can be more perilous than foreign investment, subcontracting or licensing where one firm maintains managerial and financial control. Companies here cross the line into true international collaboration with its attendant pitfalls. Traditionally seen in the chemicals, petroleum and minerals sectors, joint ventures are finding new adherents even in sectors which previously shied away from them (e.g., food products, machine tools).

International interfirm agreements have become a main focus of internationalisation strategies in the 1990s, even among firms which are competitors. These are looser, more flexible forms of international collaboration (as compared to joint ventures, licensing, subcontracting, etc.) which can be designed to suit the needs of all parties. Such alliances may be formed for research and development, production, marketing and a variety of other purposes. Surveys show that interfirm agreements are most common in aerospace, electronics and automobiles. International R&D accords are a direct outcome of the spiraling costs of research and are prevalent in high-technology sectors such as semiconductors and biotechnology. These technology alliances range from collaboration in a single point in the R&D process to complete product development and joint commercialisation. International R&D cooperation agreements among semiconductor firms mushroomed from 43 in 1983 to 90 in 1985 to over 100 in 1989.

II. TRADE AND INDUSTRIAL DEVELOPMENT

A. Developments in Trade Policy

The internationalisation of industrial activities is a main impetus to economic growth in the OECD area and takes many forms beyond the export and import of manufactures. The concept of "trade" now encompasses international transactions in services as well as global exchanges of know-how and technology. This trade is paralleled by flows of foreign investment, cross-border mergers and acquisitions and many types of international industrial collaboration. The government policy implications of these international industrial activities are discussed largely in trade policy fora, primarily the multilateral negotiations of the General Agreement for Tariffs and Trade (GATT). The topics under negotiation in successive GATT rounds reflect in part the evolution of global industrial transactions.

In the pre-war period, the OECD countries generally had high and complex tariff structures which led to excessive levels of protection in trade in manufactures. Through the establishment of the GATT in 1947 and successive rounds of GATT-sponsored trade negotiations, these tariffs were lowered substantially. By the early 1970s, tariffs had been lowered to the point that they were no longer perceived to be a dominant barrier to trade. In the 1970s, other trade-distorting practices became a main concern of the OECD countries. These included regulations, technical standards, procurement policies and other national practices which discriminated against the activities of foreign firms. These non-tariff barriers were a main subject of the Tokyo Round negotiations of the GATT held in 1973 to 1979, which attempted to reduce the importance of these impediments to trade in goods by codifying rules and procedures relating to their use.

In the early 1980s, other types of policies began to be more of a problem in international trade, including some which are largely uncovered by the GATT framework. GATT rules remain focused on trade in manufactures leaving agriculture and a large part of international industrial activities outside of GATT disciplines. Some of these activities have been included for discussion in the Uruguay Round negotiations to be concluded at yearend 1990. Measures pertaining to trade in services, trade-related investment measures and trade-related intellectual property rights measures have been added to the GATT agenda in the hope that general governing principles may be devised for their use. In addition, new policy instruments, such as grey-area measures, are being applied to traditional trade areas. GATT disciplines pertaining to subsidies and countervailing duties and dumping are to be reconsidered in the GATT Uruguay Round in light of current trends in industrial competition. Overall, trade policy approaches are taking new forms, becoming more opaque and are increasingly intertwined with domestic industrial policy measures.

B. Trade-Related Issues in Industry

Many of the industrial issues of the l980s are directly related to international trade and related transactions. These issues stem from changing patterns of trade, technology and investment and the increasing importance of service sectors and intellectual property. Table 2 shows trade-related issue areas of importance to industrial policy which have been identified in the sector case studies (see references). Most relate to government measures to modify international flows of goods and services and indicate the increasing range of issues with which industrial policymakers must cope. These policies differ by sector, but are becoming widespread across the industrial fabric as more sectors undertake diverse avenues of globalisation. International disciplines have not kept up with the evolving internationalisation of industrial activities leading to increased frictions in the multilateral trading system with implications for industrial policy.

The increasing importance of trade in **high-technology products** and direct and indirect government support to new technologies and strategic sectors have given rise to new policy concerns. Government interest in high technology sectors stems from their specific contributions to restructuring, job creation and improved balance of payments as well as the key role these industries play in the modernisation of other sectors. There is doubt that sufficient industrial growth and development can be achieved through a focus on medium and low-technology sectors or increasing incorporation of services functions. OECD governments are becoming more active in funding both basic and applied research and supporting collaborative research activities, high-technology ventures and initiatives for the commercialisation of new technologies. Despite their alleged economic advantages and desirability over many other forms of industrial intervention, R&D supports to domestic producers give them advantages in the global market and can cause frictions among trading partners. There is also fear that government support of sectors such as electronics, telecommunications and aerospace will

Table 2. **Trade-related Issues in Industry**

Area	Issue	Sector Examples
High-Technology Products	Government support to research and technology development	Aerospace Semiconductors
Trade in Services	Policies or measures which may impede services transactions	Construction Telecommunications
Foreign Investment	Rules relating to local contentor origin which may affect level of trade and investment	Auto Parts Electronics
Intellectual Property Rights	Intellectual property regimes (patent/copyright systems) which affect trade flows	Pharmaceuticals Semiconductors Computer Software
Export Financing	Government programmes to expand exports	Construction
Bilateral Trade Arrangements	Bilateral approaches to modifying trade flows in particular sectors	Semiconductors Automobiles Consumer Electronics

16

conflict with the adoption of more industry-neutral policy measures, replacing aid to traditional sectors and entailing the same risks of economic distortions.

Trade in services is increasing at a faster rate than trade in manufactures and many services sectors are confronting global competitive pressures as well as new types of trade barriers for the first time. As shown in the case study of the international construction industry, impediments to international services transactions mostly take the form of non-tariff barriers. Technical standards which favour the performance of national products and government procurement practices which give preference to domestic suppliers have formed important obstacles to internationalisation in services sectors. Prohibitions on foreign-produced advertising or films, limitations on the entry of foreign consulting or engineering companies and restrictions on foreign equity participation in retail trade activities are a few of the policies which can limit cross-border services transactions. Government requirements for some form of local presence, local hiring of personnel or local procurement of equipment can also distort services trade. Certain barriers – such as administrative inefficiencies and national regulations – may form unintentional obstacles to services imports. The OECD has for many years maintained instruments – namely the Codes of Liberalisation of Current Invisible Operations and Capital Movements and the National Treatment Instrument – to promote increased liberalisation of service transactions among OECD member countries; these codes are now being strengthened and broadened. Attempts are also being made in the GATT to develop a multilateral system of rules and disciplines aimed at liberalising trade in services.

Government policies which influence imports and exports through their effect on **foreign investment** are another controversial area in industrial trade. Under the category of trade-related investment measures (TRIMs), governments may require investors to transfer technology, conduct research and development in place, use local inputs or export a certain share of production. Governments may impose exchange restrictions on foreign companies (which limit the repatriation of capital) or requirements regarding the licensing of products and local equity participation. As shown in the case study of the automotive parts sector, many recent TRIMs have been aimed at encouraging local investment in lieu of imports in order to ameliorate trade balances and improve domestic economic performance. Controversies regarding local content in the automobile industry (requirements that a certain percentage of auto parts be locally supplied) and rules of origin in the electronics industry (requirements that photocopiers or circuit boards be not just assembled but largely originate locally) are examples. Such rules have become more problematic with the increasing internationalisation of industrial activities which makes it difficult to determine the national origin or local content of products. Progress is being made in liberalising investment flows through the OECD codes, and GATT talks are being held on strengthening rules to reduce the trade-restrictive and distortive effects of TRIMS and to improve their compatibility with principles of non-discrimination and national treatment.

Intellectual property rights have also emerged as an international issue affecting industrial development and trade. The legal protection given to the exclusive rights to certain forms of intangible property (such as inventions, designs and trademarks) are intended to encourage innovation and technology diffusion. Infringement of intellectual property is a major problem in those sectors which rely on their patents to obtain licensing income (e.g., pharmaceuticals, agro-chemicals, semiconductors) and other sectors with embodied technology or namebrands which are easy to counterfeit or pirate (e.g., computer software, clothing, records and cassettes). Government legal regimes and procedures (such as patent or copyright rules and modes of enforcement) which influence trade flows through their effects on intellectual property rights are termed trade-related intellectual property rights measures or TRIPs. International disputes regarding TRIPs can be seen in the chemicals sector, where conflicts regarding the use of patents has grown due in part to increasing trade and investment in chemicals products and the development of technology for imitating pharmaceuticals and agricultural chemicals. The case study of the chemicals industry estimates that it may account for 10 per cent of worldwide losses due to intellectual property rights infringement or US$7 to US$8 billion per year. Negotiations are being conducted in the World Intellectual Property Organisation (WIPO) on harmonising international IPR laws and in the GATT on trade-related aspects of intellectual property rights.

Although disciplines exist under OECD and GATT on the subsidisation of exports, governments still help their exporting industries through a variety of programmes and **export financing** remains a subject of international dispute. Most governments provide export credits and guarantees which allow the foreign buyer of certain goods and services to defer payment or obtain a guaranteed loan. Aid to developing countries is often tied to the purchase of goods and services in the donor country. Some governments extend mixed credits which combine export financing with development assistance in the form of low-interest loans. Importing countries may benefit from special programmes to help them buy military or infrastructure equipment, and countries may only purchase a product if they are given some part in producing it (as in offset arrangements). Government export supports may be the most important factor in the competitiveness of sectors such as international construction and are significant in sectors such as steel. For example, as shown in the case study of the international construction industry, the OECD countries have provided more than US$6 billion in tied aid and US$1 billion in mixed credits annually to construction projects in developing countries in recent years. Less tied aid and more commercially realistic terms for export financing would promote fairer international competition in many industries; this is being promoted in the OECD (through the OECD Arrangement on Guidelines for Officially Supported Export Credits) and the GATT, and frictions in the use of export credits have been resolved in several sectors as a result of these international agreements.

Bilateral trade arrangements such as voluntary export retraints (VERs) and orderly marketing agreements (OMAs), which affect the level of imports or exports in particular industrial sectors, are increasing and remain ill-defined under the GATT. For this reason, they are sometimes called grey-area measures. The narrow purpose of these measures, like that of standard tariff or non-tariff barriers, is to limit trade flows by affecting the quantities and/or prices of the goods being traded. More generally, they may be intended to counter the perceived unfair trade practices of other countries, to protect domestic industries facing import-related problems or to encourage market-opening or other types of trade actions in other countries. Semiconductors, automobiles, consumer electronics as well as steel and textiles have all been the subject of bilateral measures and they are discussed more fully in the semiconductor case study. According to the GATT, the value of total trade affected by these measures increased by over 60 per cent in the 1980s and represented more than half of the increase in all forms of government trade intervention. There are now more than 250 voluntary restraint agreements in effect, which have been largely directed towards the exports and markets of Japan and the Asian NIEs. Although such measures are often successful in promoting structural adjustment, they may incur higher costs than benefits, particularly in penalising consumers and giving monopoly profits to exporters. Proposals have been made in the GATT to make grey-area measures more transparent and subject to multilateral trade disciplines.

III. MAIN INDUSTRIAL POLICY ISSUES

A. Industrial and Trade Policy Linkages

An important feature of current OECD industrial policies is the increased linkages between industrial and trade policies. The line between industrial policies and trade policies has become blurred as these two types of government measures are increasingly interrelated in their execution and interchangeable in their effects. This policy symbiosis stems largely from the changing patterns of internationalisation of industrial activities and global competition between firms. It has important implications for the assessment of the costs and benefits of government policies and the development of new frameworks for international policy coordination.

Industrial policy has no well-defined boundaries, but generally includes those government microeconomic policies dealing with the allocation of resources among sectors and activities. Industrial policies may be directed to the distribution of resources among industries, general industrial restructuring, the regulation of natural monopolies as well as the modification of external industry costs and benefits. Common industrial policy instruments are grants, loans, tax incentives, procurement, regulation and equity participation. Industrial policy usually encompasses regional policies, research and development policies, programmes for small and medium-sized enterprises and a variety of other measures related to industry.

Industrial policy was traditionally devised and implemented with little attention to the effects on the international trading system. However, the impacts of industrial policies on global commerce gradually came to be recognised. Many industrial policies can constitute unfair trade practices or form nontariff barriers to trade at the global level. Government subsidies to industries or firms, regardless of their domestic structural purpose, reduce enterprise costs and give companies advantages in global competition. Other government policies directed to industry, including public procurement, regulations and standards, can form significant barriers to imports. GATT codes relating to subsidies and countervailing duties, standards, procurement and other areas are an attempt to mitigate the negative trade effects of industrial policies and to provide a forum for dispute settlement.

The globalisation of industrial activities has magnified the trade impacts of industrial policies and expanded the range of policies which have effects at the border. Industrial policies may now form nontariff barriers not only to trade in goods but also to flows of technology, capital and services. Patent policies, copyright systems and other aspects of domestic intellectual property regimes can distort cross-border flows of both tangible and intangible property. Investment rules, tax regimes, antitrust statutes and other business policies influence cross-border capital transactions. Government regulations are impeding the internationalisation of many services networks. Subsidies have taken on new dimensions as government supports are extended to new technologies and strategic sectors with significant trade implications. Industrial policies which received little scrutiny from trade policymakers in the past have become central to current GATT negotiations. And they tend to be more difficult to measure, monitor and coordinate than more traditional trade-related policy instruments.

Trade policy, whose boundaries are more easily defined than those of industrial policy, is distinguished by its focus on imports and exports. On the import side, traditional trade policy instruments are tariffs and quotas. On the export side, the main instruments are export financing and promotion schemes. Trade policies resemble industrial policies in that they attempt to influence the economic environment for industrial activities. In their concern with market access, trade policies and trade measures influence industrial competitiveness through their effects on cross-border flows of goods.

The expected effects of certain trade policy instruments on industrial development have long been a motivation for their use. Infant industries or favoured sectors can be protected at home from foreign competition with tariffs or quotas. Declining industries may be rejuvenated through tariff walls or quotas which provide a breathing space for structural adjustments. Production capacity in strategic sectors can be preserved through border measures. Export programmes and schemes can expand foreign markets and give national firms scale and competitive advantages. However, the validity of using trade policies for industrial development purposes has been contested and the results have not always been those originally expected.

In recent years, the effects of trade measures on industrial development have become more intricate and extensive. This is due to both the globalisation of economic activities, which has given new complexity to trade relations, and changes in the use and configuration of trade measures. Bilateral arrangements to modify trade flows in particular industrial sectors can have profound implications for industrial adjustment. Grey-area measures to restrain exports or open markets can outweigh the effects of industrial policies. Local content schemes and rules of origin can be partial determinants of domestic investment patterns. Bilateral and regional free trade agreements may be an alternative or supplement to industrial policies for enhancing industrial competitiveness.

Not only are industrial policies and trade policies no longer easily separated, their impacts are not easily isolated. Due to the globalisation of corporate activities, governments cannot be sure of the competitive effects of their industrial policies. Industrial policy measures to support domestic production may also support foreign production facilities and subsidise foreign subsidiaries. Government aids to research and development may benefit foreign firms through corporate interaction in global technology networks. Programmes to increase domestic production may subsidise goods that have largely been produced abroad through offsets and subcontracting arrangements. Investment incentives, regional policy schemes and other domestic policies may transfer income to trading partners and help strengthen rival industries.

Similarly, trade policy measures may be counteracted by the global strategies of enterprises and have unforeseen effects. Trade protectionism can cause firms to substitute investment for exports, thereby creating additional competitive pressures and even excess capacity. Bilateral arrangements to modify flows of imports and exports may encourage collusive behavior among firms and raise barriers to entry in certain sectors. Grey-area measures can foster strategic alliances among companies and lead to unintended cross-border flows of technology. Export financing schemes may support foreign subcontractors and increase competition. In general, government policies which attempt to maximise benefits to national economies are becoming more difficult to realise and sometimes counterproductive. The close linkages between trade and industrial policies must be taken into account in all government policymaking with regard to industry.

B. Evaluation of Policy Costs and Benefits

The considerable overlap between industrial and trade policies may require more systematic assessment of their impacts by OECD governments. At present, more industrial policies have trade effects and more trade measures have industrial policy effects. Governments pursuing industry-related goals are able to choose from a variety of industrial and trade policy instruments which have to a certain degree become substitutable. Both types of policies can be effective in spurring growth sectors, aiding declining industries and generally increasing industrial competitiveness. However, when used to further industrial policy goals, the costs and benefits of industrial and trade policies can vary substantially.

The use of trade policy instruments may have certain advantages in speed, flexibility and budget costs relative to traditional industrial policy approaches in improving industrial competitiveness (see Table 3). Most trade measures are viewed as short-term stop-gap actions either to correct situations of unfair trade or to provide sectors with time to adjust to international competition. Many trade policy measures, particularly newer instruments such as grey-area measures which are not subject to GATT disciplines, can be rapidly implemented; they are thus more easily used than industrial policy solutions in dealing with competitive pressures. Their costs to governments are generally low and measures such as tariffs can be sources of revenue. The effects of trade measures in improving industrial performance relative to competing imports or exports are usually immediate.

Table 3.   **General Comparison of Trade Policy and Industrial Policy**

Criteria	Trade Policy	Industrial Policy
Purpose	Influence trade flows	Improve industry competitiveness
Method	Limit imports/increase exports	Facilitate industrial adjustment
Instruments	Tariffs, quotas, export schemes	Subsidies, taxes, procurement, regulation
Variety	Traditionally a limited number of measures	Wider selection of instruments
Speed	Many are rapid and flexible	Often slower and less flexible
Budget Cost	Lower budget costs	High budget costs
Consumer Cost	High consumer cost	High taxpayer cost
Effectiveness	Relatively shorter-term effects	Possible longer-term effects
Rules	Guided by national and often by regional and international rules	Guided by national or regional rules; generally not guided by international rules

In contrast, industrial policy approaches such as grants, loans, tax incentives and consultancy schemes generally have long lead-times, long pay-off periods and high budget costs in promoting industrial adjustment. The costs to the public of both types of policies may be relatively equal, although these costs are often direct in the case of industrial policies (through the effect on taxes) and indirect in the case of trade policies (through the effect on prices). Because many industrial policies are not subject to international rules or disciplines, they may ultimately pose more of a threat to the stability of the multilateral trading system than trade policies.

Due to their combined impacts and overlapping usage, assessment of industrial and trade policies is best conducted in unison just as these approaches are best used as complements in promoting industrial adjustment. Some problems attributed to the weaknesses of domestic industrial policies or adjustment processes may actually call for trade policy solutions due to their root cause in the unfair trade practices of other countries or in global market failures. For example, industrial subsidies or R&D funding may not compensate for consistent dumping of products in domestic markets by foreign competitors. Poor industrial performance in world markets may be due to trade barriers or high levels of competitive export financing. Policy interventions may be warranted to counter market imperfections linked to the existence of external oligopolies or the need for global-scale economies in production or research.

Similarly, some industrial difficulties imputed to the trading system may necessitate industrial policy corrections. Increased capital investments in plant and equipment or intangible investments in training and research may be more advantageous to troubled industries in the long-term than tariffs or bilateral trade restraints. Rationalisation and retraining may be more applicable to improving competitiveness in some sectors than trade policies or border measures. The challenge to governments is to establish whether trade and/or industrial policy interventions are demanded and how these policy instruments may be used together to promote longer-term adaptation of industries to global competitive pressures.

OECD governments are beginning to conduct regular assessments of industrial and trade policies. Some OECD countries have developed mechanisms for evaluating the industrial impacts of public assistance programs, although such efforts are not widespread or systematic. Cross-policy evaluations including trade policies and sectoral assessments of policy approaches are still rare. The Industry Committee reviewed the status of assessment of industrial policies including methodological aspects in a recent theme discussion (see references). The need to develop and apply new methodologies for policy assessment, particularly for the quantification of relative costs and benefits, was underlined. In addition, increasing attention is being given to the review of microeconomic policies and their structural adjustment implications in the OECD Economic Surveys of Member countries.

In 1988, the GATT initiated a Trade Policy Review Mechanism to conduct country assessments of government trade policies and their impact on the multilateral trading system; these trade policy reviews are not generally focused on policy effectiveness. Many industrial policies are not covered by the GATT code and may escape consideration. The cross-policy effects of industrial and trade policies may not be fully taken into account. Few evaluations at the sectoral level are conducted, yet the evaluation of the combined impacts of industrial and trade policies may best be assessed within the context of industrial sectors. Efforts to improve the transparency of industrial and trade policies (as is now being done in the Industry Committee project on Subsidies and Structural Adjustment) and to compare their use and advantages in achieving structural adjustment objectives may need to be increased at both the national and international levels.

C. Industrial Policy and Globalisation

The globalisation of industrial activities and overlaps between industrial and trade policies may necessitate a broader multilateral framework for harmonisation of industrial policies. A third phase of internationalisation has been reached which comprises trade, foreign investment and global networking; this globalisation implies a move beyond mere interdependence to the mixing and blending of national economies, largely due to the activities of multinational enterprises. Policy areas which were previously considered domestic now have spillover effects on the welfare of other countries and implications for the world trading system.

Global enterprise strategies also demand new approaches to the design and implementation of government policies and programmes. As illustrated in the sector case studies, a global economic system is emerging whose primary agents are transnational corporations linked through enterprise networks. Many industrial and trade policies are counteracted by the global activities of firms who seek competitive advantages in different countries. OECD governments often compete to attract the attention of these transnational actors while working to preserve the highest value-added activities at home. The foot-loose character of international industry combined with the inherent nationalistic tendencies of governments may call for redirection as well as harmonisation of industrial policies.

The international coordination of macroeconomic policies among OECD countries has progressed considerably as has that of many trade-related policies. Now more industrial policies are raising questions regarding the need for greater convergence to reduce international frictions and assure global economic growth. However, such coordination in the case of these microeconomic policies may be far more difficult owing to the greater range and diversity of measures and the problems in monitoring their effects. OECD governments need to explore avenues of cooperation across a broad spectrum of policy areas, including those pertaining to industrial supports, technology, competition, foreign investment and intellectual property.

Industrial subsidies to create competitive advantages for national firms are one source of international frictions. Traditional trade barriers have been reduced, while certain industrial subsidies have increased in trade importance as countries seek to attain international economic advantages. Current trade disciplines relating to subsidies are widely considered inadequate and are being discussed in the GATT, while the OECD has undertaken efforts to increase the transparency of subsidies in the Industry Committee and in the Committee on International Investment and Multinational Enterprises (CIME) and in other contexts relating to export credits, agriculture, shipbuilding and steel. These constitute initial steps towards international harmonisation of the main instrument of industrial policy.

National **technology policies** can be discordant and counterproductive in the current global industrial environment. Governments may need to explore the benefits of greater cooperation in devising R&D approaches in order to mitigate emerging technology frictions. Technology initiatives that ignore the increasing international interdependence of research and development may be ineffective. The competitive subsidisation of a few high-technology or strategic sectors suggests the possibility of globally excessive and duplicative resources dedicated to some activities. Policies to isolate and build technology through domestic strategies may slow progress by reducing the scale of the market and blocking the cross-fertilisation of ideas. New international codes may be warranted regarding the government role in supporting R&D, commercialising technology and providing mutual access to government-sponsored research.

The globalisation of industrial activities has raised new questions of **competition policy.** Internationalisation through networking has been practiced mostly by large firms from the major OECD countries in certain industrial sectors. Through their international alliances, some firms have formed groupings that would be impossible in domestic markets due to antitrust and competition policies. Government attempts to enhance competitiveness through the creation of industrial consortia are leading to a broader interpretation of competition rules. Developments in trade policy, such as bilateral export restraints, can act to concentrate industries and foster the emergence of cartels. The application of national competition rules to the activities of foreign firms and their subsidiaries is another uncertain area. Multilateral appoaches to competition policy may be needed to ensure the maintenance of competitive conditions worldwide. Guidelines could help lower barriers to entry which might hinder participation in global industrial networks by smaller countries and firms and latecomers.

Increasing **foreign investment** and government policy responses have prompted predictions that trade frictions may be replaced by investment frictions in the 1990s. The overwhelming trend in recent years has been towards greater liberalisation of investment flows in the OECD countries. Yet recent calls, however narrowly-based, for erecting controls on foreign investment may indicate a need for increased transparency and coordination of policies. Some countries are concerned about the hollowing out of their productive base as multinationals move activities and technology abroad. Other countries are seeking to ensure that multinationals act as good corporate citizens in their adopted bases of operation. In some cases, government incentives to foreign investment are coming into direct conflict with disincentives. Restrictive investment measures often result from a spillover of problems in the trade area and can lead to distortions in the application of GATT rules. As investment controls are targeted to particular sectors and sources of investment, GATT and OECD foreign investment disciplines may need to be strengthened to ensure ''managed investment'' is not a counterpart to managed trade.

International **intellectual property rights** regimes and enforcement could enhance global technology development and dissemination. IPR rules can be used to stimulate technological progress as well as to influence trade and investment flows. Variations in the scope, duration and other features of OECD systems and the shortcomings of international conventions in bridging these differences reduce the economic returns to industries and the incentives to conduct research. Firms encounter problems in many non-OECD countries whose intellectual property systems may be explicitly designed to encourage technology transfer. Rules regarding newer forms of intangible property as embodied in computer software, semiconductors or biotechnology need to be devised. Harmonisation of OECD intellectual property codes, including those relating to frontier technology areas, could lessen the need for policy interventions to remedy research deficiencies and promote fairer industrial competition.

In summary, multilateral approaches to industrial policies may be essential to reducing conflicts in the international system and ensuring future industrial growth. Government attempts to create competitive advantages for domestic industries have led to conflicting industrial policies which will not be well tolerated in an increasingly global system. Greater convergence of industrial policies would reduce system tensions and lessen possible asymmetries in access to trade, technology and investment. Industrial policymakers may need to formulate new multilateral rules to ensure that competition between governments does not replace competition between enterprises in an era of globalisation of industrial activities. First steps towards implementing this process may be defining problem areas, identifying where international harmonisation is possible and proposing general frameworks for co-operation.

REFERENCES

Chesnais, F. (1988) ''Technical Co-Operation Agreements Between Firms'', *STI Review* No. 4, OECD, Paris, December.

De Bandt, J. (1987), ''Des mesures combinées de politique commerciale et de politique industrielle: tendance ou non au protectionisme?'', *Economies et Sociétés,* April.

Michalet, C.A. (1989), ''Global Competition and its Implications for Firms'', International Seminar on Science, Technology and Economic Growth, OECD, May.

Mowery, D.C. (1989), ''Collaborative Ventures between U.S. and Foreign Manufacturing Firms'', *Research Policy,* 18.

OECD (1990), ''Assessment of Industrial Policies: Methodological Aspects and Examples from Member Countries'', Paris, March.

Ostry, S. (1990), *Governments and Corporations in a Shrinking World,* Council on Foreign Relations, New York.

CASE OF STUDY

THE AUTOMOTIVE PARTS INDUSTRY

I. SUMMARY

The automotive parts sector, previously treated as a subsector of the automobile industry, has emerged in the 1980s as an important industry in its own right. OECD automotive parts firms are confronting severe adjustment pressures partly as a result of intense competition in the automobile industry. Many OECD automakers are now restructuring their relationships with auto parts suppliers to improve efficiency. Automakers are also requiring that their auto parts suppliers act quickly to increase quality, improve delivery systems, reduce costs and assume greater responsibility for product design and technology development. The automotive parts industry is attempting to meet these mandates in an environment of slow demand growth and potential overcapacity.

International competition in automotive parts is intensifying as trade and foreign investment reach new highs within the OECD area. The volume of OECD trade in auto parts has expanded three-fold since 1979. Japanese firms have increased their market share in auto parts to equal that of the United States due to the strength of Japan's automobile sales, a cohesive industry structure and advantages in quality, delivery and design. US and European automakers are increasing their outside purchases of auto parts from both domestic and foreign sources to maximise quality and value. Foreign investment in parts production is growing, particularly by Japanese firms seeking to locate near Japanese automakers abroad and provide a hedge against exchange rate fluctuations and potential trade barriers. There are now about 150 Japanese auto parts facilities in North America and many firms are considering investment in the European countries.

The following are the major policy issues identified:

a) *Global Firm Strategies and Industrial Policies:* International competition is accelerating in automotive parts due to trade, foreign investment and technological trends. Auto parts firms need new global strategies and, although these should be developed in response to market developments, may look to governments for assistance in restructuring, technology development and improving competitiveness.

b) *Local Content Rules:* National policies requiring or encouraging certain levels of local parts content in automobile assembly are intended to realize the full positive effects of foreign investment on local economies and have developed in response to changing relationships between manufacturers and parts suppliers. However, governments need to agree on rules for the use of these measures in the GATT.

c) *Foreign Investment Issues:* In order for the positive effects of foreign investment in the OECD area to be fully realised, Japanese automakers need to make greater attempts to integrate foreign parts firms into their supply networks at home and abroad. Other OECD governments need to avoid excessive use of incentives and disincentives to foreign investment, which can cause trade and investment distortions.

29

II. INDUSTRY BACKGROUND

A. Product Structure

Information and statistics on automotive parts traditionally have been subsumed under the automobile or motor vehicle industry. In the 1980s, the globalisation and intensification of competition in automotive parts has led to their consideration as a separate manufacturing sector. However, the automotive parts sector remains difficult to define; essentially, it consists of firms which produce goods used in the production of automobiles. The range of products which they produce is diverse and includes carburetors, pistons, rings, lighting equipment, transmissions, brakes, batteries, body parts and seats. These products include original equipment (OE) parts (for assembly into new cars or for dealer service operations) and parts for the aftermarket (replacement parts for vehicles repaired by independent facilities).

Automotive parts account for on average 60 per cent of the manufacturing cost of an automobile, the remainder being assembly including painting and tooling. These parts can be grouped into five general categories with their average contribution to total component cost: engine and transmission parts (30 per cent), chassis or frame (23 per cent), miscellaneous accessories and parts (21 per cent), exterior body parts (16 per cent) and electrical systems (10 per cent). It is forecast that the share of electrical components, which may eventually be mass produced, will continue to grow. The use of new materials and new process and product technologies should also influence these shares. Engine and transmission parts are the highest value-added components followed by the basic auto frame or chassis. The product structure of automotive parts output varies by country due partly to foreign investment and regional trade in parts (see Table 4). It should be noted that all comparative statistics on automotive parts must be interpreted with caution due to the lack of a standard definition of the automotive parts sector and its subsectors.

B. Industry Structure

Compared to the automobile industry, which is characterised by an oligopolistic supply structure, the automotive parts industry is far less concentrated. The production of automobiles is the domain of a few firms in the major OECD countries. US production is dominated by General Motors, Ford and Chrysler; Japan's two largest firms, Toyota and Nissan, account for about 50 per cent of Japan's auto output; production by European firms is concentrated in a few national champions. On a global scale, the top ten automobile firms account for about 75 per cent of total production. In contrast, the top 30 automotive parts firms account for about a third of world production (see Table 5).

31

Table 4. **Product Structure of Automotive Parts Production: 1986**

Percentages

	United States	Japan	Germany	France	Italy	Canada
Engine Parts	31.0	23.0	20.0	14.0	13.0	31.0
Chassis	30.0	22.0	20.0	53.0	21.0	10.0
Accessories	20.0	32.0	41.0	2.0	19.0	26.0
Body Parts	12.0	15.0	4.0	15.0	20.0	20.0
Electrical	7.0	8.0	15.0	16.0	27.0	13.0
Total	100.0	100.0	100.0	100.0	100.0	100.0

Source: Adapted from national sources.

The structure of the auto parts industry in most OECD countries is characterised by a small number of large firms and a large number of small and medium-sized enterprises (SMEs). There are basically three types of auto parts firms: *i)* the large diversified producers whose output consists of many products in addition to auto parts (e.g., Mitsubishi Electric in Japan, Bosch and Siemens in Germany, Allied Signal, TRW and Rockwell in the United States, GKN and Lucas in the United Kingdom); *ii)* the larger producers specialising in auto parts (e.g., Nippon Denso in Japan, Dana and Eaton in the United States, Valeo in France, Magnetti Marelli in Italy); and *iii)* the thousands of SMEs producing auto parts on a smaller scale.

Japan's auto parts industry is characterised by a unique pyramidal structure, topped off by the largest 300 firms which supply components and subassemblies directly to the automobile manufacturers. These are the firms which make up the Japan Auto Parts Industry Association (JAPIA) and include Aisin Seiki, Nihon Radiator, Toyoda Gosei, Diesel Kiki and Atsugi Motor. Many of the larger component suppliers began as subsidiaries of the Japanese automakers; about 18 per cent of these firms – such as Nippon Denso – remain affiliated suppliers (more than 20 per cent owned by the automakers). Below this level of companies, there are about 10 000 SMEs organised in second and third tiers which supply auto parts to the larger subassemblers.

The North American and European automobile industries traditionally have been more vertically integrated than the Japanese industry, with most suppliers under the total or partial equity control of the automakers. These sectors are being gradually decentralised resulting in the rise of a number of large independent auto parts producers. In the United States and Canada, the affiliated auto parts producers of General Motors, Ford and Chrysler (Acustar) still account for about 40 per cent of domestic sales. Independent US firms with 2 per cent or more of the auto parts market include Allied Signal, Dana, Borg-Warner, TRW and Rockwell. In addition, there are some 15 000 SMEs in the US industry most with product specialities. A few of the medium-range US companies have recently acquired an international dimension in their specialty through acquisitions and foreign investment: Johnson Controls (seats), Sheller-Globe (seats and plastic parts) and Champion and Federal-Mogul (aftermarket parts).

The European auto parts industry is also made up of a few large multinationals and many smaller firms; more than 55 per cent of European auto parts firms are SMEs with less than 100 employees. In Germany, there are 400 larger auto parts firms led by Bosch, which is the largest unaffiliated auto parts producer in the world and a leader in the field of electronic

Table 5. **Principal Automotive Parts Manufacturers: 1987**

	Company headquarters	Estimated sales (mil US$)	Total world market share (%)
General Motors	US	24 000	10.9
Nippon Denso	Japan	8 500	3.9
Bosch	Germany	7 500	3.4
Allied Signal	US	3 500	1.6
Dana	US	3 000	1.4
Valeo	France	2 700	1.2
Mitsubishi Electric	Japan	2 400	1.1
ITT	US	2 200	1.0
Aisin Seiki	Japan	2 200	1.0
Lucas	UK	2 000	0.9
Magnetti Marelli	Italy	2 000	0.9
GKN	UK	1 800	0.8
Mitsubishi Heavy	Japan	1 800	0.8
Nippon Seiko	Japan	1 700	0.8
Borg Warner	US	1 500	0.7
Rockwell	US	1 500	0.7
Eaton	US	1 500	1.7
TRW	US	1 500	1.7
Varity	US	1 500	0.7
ZF	Germany	1 200	0.5
Nihon Radiator	Japan	1 100	0.5
Toyoda Gosei	Japan	1 000	0.5
Diesel Kiki	Japan	1 000	0.5
Johnson Controls	US	1 000	0.5
Fichtel und Sachs	Germany	1 000	0.5
IC-Industries	US	1 000	0.5
Magna	Canada	1 000	0.5
VDO	Germany	950	0.4
Siemens	Germany	900	0.4
Atsugi Motor	Japan	800	0.4
NHK	Japan	700	0.3
Pacific Dunlop	Australia	110	0.1
Total	32 firms	81 500	36.5

Source: J.J. Chanaron (1988).

injection and braking systems. France, which has about 350 auto parts firms supplying the domestic auto companies Renault and Peugeot, has one company of international size – Valeo, the second largest European auto parts producer after Bosch. Valeo has been partially controlled by the Italian Benedetti group since 1986. Other leading French auto parts firms are Epeda-Bertrand-Faure and ECIA.

Italy's auto parts sector of about 250 firms is dominated by Fiat which owns in whole or in part many of the parts suppliers through its holding company Fiat Componenti (e.g., Weber, Borletti, Fiat Lubricanti, Gilardini, Comind). Fiat also owns 55 per cent of Magnetti Marelli, the third largest European auto parts company, which is diversifying through taking holdings in other European companies such as France's Solex (Matra), Jaeger and Valeo. In the United Kingdom, most of the large firms (e.g., Lucas, GKN, Turner and Newall, BTR, TI Engineering) have internationalised to reduce dependence on the internal market, which is also supplied by a large number of SMEs. Australia's largest auto parts firm, Pacific Dunlop, has also had impressive growth in sales in recent years.

C. Demand Trends

The auto parts industry supplies two principal markets: the original equipment (OE) parts market and the aftermarket. Demand for OE parts accounts for an average 60 per cent to 65 per cent of auto parts sales in the OECD area, making demand for auto parts highly dependent on demand for automobiles.

The steady growth in demand for automobiles and auto parts enjoyed in the 1960s and early 1970s changed markedly with the two oil shocks in 1973 and 1979. Demand declined in North America and Japan after 1973 and slowed considerably in Europe (see Table 6). Continuing very low growth rates in demand indicate that OECD automobile markets have approached saturation. The three major automobile markets – Europe, North America and Japan, which absorb about 85 per cent of world production – offer limited expansion opportunities. This is despite record level automobile sales in 1988. Non-OECD markets in Africa, Asia and Latin America have a higher rate of demand growth, but their share of total automobile consumption is still small and is increasingly supplied from domestic capacity.

Most forecasts predict a 2 per cent average annual increase in the world automobile market over the next ten years and between 1.5 per cent and 2 per cent demand growth in the OECD area. Low growth in demand has put increasing pressure for structural adjustment on both the automobile industry and the auto parts sector. There are forecasts of overcapacity in automobile production in the 1990s due to excessive investment in the major OECD countries and the emergence of new competitors in non-OECD countries. In the auto parts sector, slow demand growth has prompted restructuring of companies, greater diversification of products and markets and increasing reliance on the sale of replacement parts to the aftermarket.

Table 6. **Trends in OECD Automobile Demand**[1]

Percentages

	1965-1973	1973-1979	1979-1986	1987-1993
North America	2.6	−0.6	0.6	1.3
Japan	24.5	−0.5	1.2	1.7
Europe	5.4	1.7	1.7	1.8
Total	5.0	0.3	1.1	1.6

1. Average annual percentage change in new car registrations.
Source: GERPISA.

D. Production and Employment Trends

The automobile industry, including components, accounts for between 5 and 10 per cent of manufacturing production and employment in the major OECD automobile producing countries. In most countries, the production of automotive parts accounts for 50 per cent or more of the total. Table 7 gives estimates of the value of world auto parts production according to geographic location; however, these figures may not be entirely accurate owing to country variations in the definition of the auto parts sector, exchange rate movements and other statistical difficulties.

The OECD accounts for almost all world production of auto parts, although producers in Korea, Brazil and other non-OECD countries are increasing their share of output. The United States and Japan are the world's largest auto parts producers, with their industries following the evolution of their automobile sectors. The US auto parts industry reached a peak in industry shipments in 1978, suffered a decline through 1982 but has since experienced a recovery. Since 1983, growth in US automotive parts production is due to increased out-sourcing (purchases from other firms) by US automobile companies, an upswing in the aftermarket and increased production by foreign firms locating in the United States.

Table 7. **Trends in Automotive Parts Production**[1]

	1983		1987	
	Value (mil. $)	Share (%)	Value (mil. $)	Share (%)
United States	67 600	37.5	94 500	38.0
Japan	56 500	31.4	81 800	33.0
Europe	47 000	26.0	57 500	23.0
Germany	15 320	8.5	26 500	10.7
France	10 720	5.9	10 800	4.3
United Kingdom	5 500	3.0	7 200	2.8
Italy	6 160	3.4	5 000	2.0
Spain	1 980	1.1	6 300	2.5
Belgium	n.a.	n.a.	800	0.3
Portugal	320	0.1	720	0.1
Canada	7 000	4.0	10 700	4.2
Australia	n.a.	n.a.	1 870	0.1
Total OECD	178 100	99.0	247 000	98.2
Non-OECD	2 000	1.0	4 500	1.8
Korea	930	0.6	2 500	1.1
Taiwan	330	0.2	750	0.3
Total world	180 100	100.0	252 000	100.0

n.a. = not available.
1. Automotive parts sales in current US dollars based on location of production.
Source: OECD estimates.

Table 8.   **Automotive Parts Employment**

In thousand

	1979	1983	1987
United States	728	547	670
Japan	468	488	530
Germany	225	227	240
France	141	119	102
United Kingdom	214	139	125
Italy	n.a.	48	46
Canada	n.a.	60	68
Australia	n.a.	n.a.	25

n.a. = not available.
Source: Based on national sources.

Japanese auto parts producers have profited from the performance of their automobile industry to achieve international status and sales. The market share of the Japanese auto parts industry is believed to almost equal that of the United States, although firms from both countries have located a portion of production abroad. In Europe, Germany's auto parts industry has increased it share of world production since 1983, while France, the United Kingdom and Italy have experienced a decline in market share. At present, the European auto parts industry is restructuring in anticipation of increased foreign competition and the removal of barriers in the European market.

Employment in the auto parts sector has evidenced very slow growth or declines in most of the producing countries in the last decade (see Table 8). Employment was at its peak in 1979 with about 2 million persons employed in auto parts production worldwide. Between 1979 and 1982, about 200 000 people left the industry due to the severity of the automotive recession and industry attempts at rationalisation. As demand recovered after 1983, overall employment in the OECD auto parts sector again increased. Of the major producing countries, only Japan and Germany have shown steady but slow growth in employment in the auto parts sector.

Automation, modernisation and rationalisation in North America and several European countries resulted in a marked reduction in auto parts employment after 1979. The United Kingdom has had the most severe continuing decrease in employment, while auto parts employment in both the United States and Canada picked up again in 1983. France and Italy have experienced continued decreases in employment in this sector. Most countries have significantly increased productivity in auto parts production due to new automated production technologies as well as consolidation and restructuring. Japan has set the standards for worker productivity in automotive parts production as well as in automobile assembly.

E.   Trade and Foreign Investment Trends

The volume of trade in automotive parts in the OECD area has increased approximately three-fold between 1979 and 1987. The need to locate production close to national markets is in part responsible for the development of OECD commerce in automotive parts, subassemblies

Table 9.   **OECD Automotive Parts Trade**

	Year	Trade balance (mil US$)	Import penetration[1] (%)	Export share[2] (%)
United States	1987	-7 190	18.3	12.1
Japan	1986/87	8 120	0.6	16.8
United Kingdom[3]	1987	-1 460	35.0	30.0
Germany[3]	1986	9 100	9.0	35.0
France[3]	1987	3 400	16.0	30.0
Italy[3]	1986	1 200	24.0	40.0
Canada	1986	-5 300	73.0	64.0

1. Imports as a share of domestic consumption.
2. Exports as a share of production.
3. Includes intra-EEC trade.
Source: Adapted from national sources.

and kits as a substitute for fully assembled vehicles. Other factors contributing to the increase in auto parts trade include foreign investment in automobile production, greater outside purchases and foreign sourcing of components by OECD automakers and the role of technologies, such as the use of platforms, in reducing the need for scale economies in automobile assembly. An estimated 45 per cent of OECD trade in automotive parts is intra-firm trade, although this share is now decreasing with more out-sourcing by automakers.

US trade in auto parts has traditionally been dominated by trade with Canada due to their closely integrated automobile industries. However, Canada's share of US auto parts imports has decreased as imports from Japan and Mexico have grown. The US deficit in auto parts trade, first registered in 1984, increased to over $7 billion in 1987 (see Table 9). US automobile manufacturers are sourcing more OE parts from foreign companies or subsidiaries abroad, while Japanese assemblers located in the United States obtain the bulk of their major components from Japan. It is estimated that US automakers now import about 12 per cent of their components, while Japanese automakers located in the United States import more than 50 per cent of their parts. The United States registers its largest trade deficit with Japan.

European trade in auto parts is largely intra-European as parts are transferred between countries, partly by foreign assemblers such as Ford and General Motors. Approximately 10 to 12 per cent of European production is exported to the United States and less than 1 per cent to Japan; overall EEC auto parts trade with the rest of the world was in surplus by about $7 billion in 1987. Germany, which exports about 35 per cent of its auto parts production, accounts for 60 per cent of EEC exports outside Europe and registers a continuing trade surplus. In intra-EEC trade, Germany, France and Italy have surpluses in auto parts while the United Kingdom, Belgium and the Netherlands register deficits. Auto parts trade of other EEC countries – Ireland, Denmark, Spain, Greece and Portugal – is practically in balance. Austria, which exports engines and transmissions, maintains a trade surplus.

Japan has the lowest rate of import penetration in auto parts trade and a continuing surplus on its auto parts account. While US and European firms have had difficulties in their attempts to supply OE parts to Japanese automobile manufacturers for use in cars produced in Japan, recent attempts have met with more success. Their efforts to supply the aftermarket for Japanese auto parts in Japan and other countries have been somewhat limited by structural

Table 10. **Foreign Investment in Auto Parts in the United States**

Annual Growth Rates

	Japanese Firms	European Firms
1980	4.1	9.5
1981	1.0	10.8
1982	6.7	10.8
1983	7.7	18.9
1984	8.8	9.5
1985	16.0	10.8
1986	17.5	8.1
1987	23.2	10.3
1988	15.0	1.4

Source: Ward's Auto World.

relationships between Japanese firms. Japanese auto parts exports are primarily to North America and Asia and to a lesser extent, Europe.

Foreign investment in auto parts has generally followed the pattern of foreign investment in the automobile industry. American auto parts firms were the first to internationalise production in the 1950s and 1960s to supply Ford and General Motors plants in Europe. They later invested in facilities to supply parts to US assembly operations in Latin America, primarily Brazil, Mexico and Argentina. European auto parts firms first invested outside local markets in the early 1970s, primarily in Spain and Yugoslavia, and somewhat later in the United States and Latin American countries. US and European auto parts firms have primarily joint ventures and licensing arrangements in Asian countries such as Korea and Taiwan.

The most remarkable foreign investment trend has been the internationalisation of Japanese parts suppliers since the beginning of the 1980s, particularly in the United States and Canada. Previously located domestically, Japanese parts suppliers have followed Japanese automakers in setting up facilities in North America, in part to provide a hedge against fluctuations in exchange rates and potential trade barriers. In addition, many suppliers have been offered investment incentives by local authorities and gain competitive advantages by close proximity to Japanese assemblers who have encouraged parts suppliers to locate near their North American plants.

The number of Japanese auto parts suppliers operating facilities in the United States has grown rapidly since the appreciation of the yen in 1985 (see Table 10). Of the 290 foreign parts companies with facilities in the United States, about 150 are Japanese with the remainder European and Canadian. Foreign firms are estimated to account for slightly more than 10 per cent of US auto parts production in 1988. Japanese auto parts firms are expected to continue to set up plants within a narrow radius of Japanese assembly facilities in North America. It is estimated that about a fourth of the Japanese auto parts makers in the United States are subsidiaries of Japanese automakers, another fourth are in joint ventures with US auto parts companies and many others are cooperatives bringing together several Japanese SMEs. Japanese firms have recently begun marketing efforts to sell auto parts to US automobile manufacturers and in the aftermarket for both US and foreign cars.

Table 11. **Foreign Investment in Automotive Parts Production:**
1988

Percentages

	Production Share of Foreign Firms[1] (%)
United States	> 10
Japan	< 1
France	> 50
Germany	< 20
United Kingdom	> 30
Italy	< 10
Spain	> 85
Canada	> 80
Australia	> 70

1. Firms with headquarters in another country.
Source: J.J. Chanaron (1988).

Very few foreign auto parts firms have located in Japan, and those that have – Garrett, TRW, GKN and Michelin – are generally the larger multinationals with high-technology operations. In Canada, domestic ownership of the auto parts industry increased from about 4 per cent in the 1970s to over 16 per cent at present due to the growth of Canadian companies such as Magna International. Japanese parts firms now have 23 operations in Canada, of which 12 are joint ventures. Hyundai's new Canadian assembly plant will be the first foreign investment by a Korean automobile manufacturer and investment by Korean parts producers may follow.

Foreign investment in Europe by Japanese firms in automobile assembly and parts production is not expected to grow as rapidly as in North America. However, Japanese auto parts producers are increasing their investment in Europe, initially to supply Nissan plants in the United Kingdom and Spain and the collaborative projects of Honda and Rover. US auto parts producers remain the largest investors in Europe, accounting for about a fifth of European auto parts production while Japanese firms still account for less than 1 per cent. The share of foreign auto parts producers varies by country, with France and Spain having the highest foreign investment ratio (see Table 11). Extensive investment by OECD automakers has made Spain the fourth largest car producer in Europe and a large producer of components. Foreign investment in the auto parts industries of Italy and Germany remains relatively low.

III. MAJOR COMPETITIVE FACTORS

A. Automobile Industry Performance

The competitiveness of auto parts sectors is largely dependent on the performance of the automobile industry to which they are linked. The fortunes of auto parts firms can rise and fall with the fate of those manufacturers to which they sell original equipment parts. Increased competition in the automobile industry and changing patterns of production and trade have put pressures on auto parts firms to restructure, relocate and meet the increasing demands of automobile manufacturers engaged in a battle for market share.

The profile of automobile production has changed since the 1960s, when output was dominated by firms from five OECD countries – the United States, United Kingdom, France, Germany and Italy. Japanese companies increased their market share from less than 2 per cent in 1970 to more than 25 per cent in 1988 to become major competitors. Firms from non-OECD countries, particularly Korea, also increased their share of world output and may account for more than 16 per cent of production by 2000 (see Table 12). In terms of the geographic location of production, Western Europe remains in the top spot followed by North America and Japan. It is forecast that an increasing number of the vehicles sold in North America and Western Europe will be built there, while the number of vehicles built in Japan will decrease.

US automobile producers began losing market share after the oil shocks of the 1970s when demand increased for smaller, more fuel-efficient vehicles of the types manufactured in Japan and Europe. The increase in the value of the dollar in 1980 further weakened the competitive position of the US automobile industry. Demand for imported cars grew from less than 8 per cent of the US market in 1973 to 20 per cent in 1980 and to about 25 per cent in recent years. Foreign automakers (both imports and US based) accounted for 33 per cent of the US automobile market in 1987 and Japanese producers alone for 24 per cent. Due to these trends, US auto parts firms have seen a decline in their market for OE parts with little prospect of offsetting this through increased sales to foreign assemblers in North America.

European automobile producers also have declining world market share, with German and Italian producers faring better than those in the United Kingdom and France. US firms account for approximately 22 per cent of automobile sales in Europe almost entirely through local production. Japanese firms, which hold 11 per cent of the European market entirely through exports, are constrained by import restrictions and have recently started to produce cars there. In unrestricted markets such as Sweden, Belgium and the Netherlands, Japanese automobiles have captured more than 20 per cent of the market. In general, European volume automobile producers have struggled in the 1980s to reduce breakeven levels and maintain profitability while investing in new facilities and models. Many of the more specialised producers, such as Volvo, Saab, BMW and Porsche, have had fewer difficulties. Parts suppliers have benefited

41

Table 12. **Trends in World Automobile Production**[1]

Percentages

	Production by Firm Headquarters			Production by Region		
	1985	1990	2000	1985	1990	2000
North America	38.2	36.6	33.9	28.7	29.4	29.2
Japan	24.8	26.5	27.8	23.7	19.0	17.5
Western Europe	28.0	26.2	22.1	34.8	37.4	37.9
Eastern and central European countries	7.3	7.7	9.6	7.3	7.7	9.6
Others	1.7	3.0	6.6	5.5	6.5	5.8
Total	100.0	100.0	100.0	100.0	100.0	100.0

1. Share of units produced.
Source: Economist Intelligence Unit (1988).

from a somewhat sheltered market but fear increased competition in the 1990s, when Japanese firms may begin automobile and parts production in volume in Europe.

Japan's major automobile producers – Toyota, Nissan, Honda, Mazda and Mitsubishi – compete fiercely in a domestic market which they dominate but which is becoming rapidly saturated. Foreign cars, mostly European, account for about 4 per cent of the Japanese market. Japan exports about half of automobile output and all of the major producers now have production facilities in North America. Japan's rapid increase in world market share has been partly due to the advantages provided by an undervalued yen and a strategy of producing lower-cost, mass-produced subcompacts. Japan's automobile success has extended to its auto parts producers, who profit from expanding automobile production and sales worldwide and also the growing aftermarket for Japanese auto parts.

B. Assembler-Supplier Relationships

A main competitive factor in the auto parts industry is the nature of the relationship with the automobile industry to which it is linked. The unique structure of the Japanese auto parts sector and its close ties with Japan's automobile producers has contributed to both its success in foreign locales and its close hold on the domestic Japanese market. Japan's auto parts industry is distinguished by its low level of vertical integration, pyramidal structure and close collaboration with Japanese automobile firms.

In comparison with the American and European industry, Japan's automobile producers are more dependent on outside auto parts suppliers than on inhouse production of parts. The level of vertical integration is the lowest of the major OECD countries; Japan's automobile firms get only about 20 per cent of their parts from inhouse suppliers compared to 40 to 50 per cent for many other producers (see Table 13). The US, German and Italian car industries have traditionally made half their parts internally, while UK automobile producers have relied more on independent domestic parts producers. In the past two or three years, US and European automakers have increased their outside purchases of auto parts from other firms in the attempt to gain higher quality for lower cost.

The Japanese auto parts industry is organised in a vertical tier-like system or pyramid with the auto producers at the top and first, second and third tier parts suppliers below. The first tier firms are generally subcontractors who provide major components or subassemblies such as engines, instrument panels and suspension systems. The second and third tier suppliers provide the parts needed for the production of the larger components or systems. As a result, Japanese automakers deal with fewer auto parts firms than their OECD counterparts. Japanese automobile producers have direct business relationships with only the top 200 to 300 suppliers, while US and European producers may typically deal with some 1 000 to 2 000 auto parts companies.

Table 13.   **Trends in Vertical Integration in the Automobile Industry[1]**

Percentages

Country/Company	1968	1978	1983	1985
United States:				
General Motors	52.8	48.0	50.5	50.0
Ford	38.3	39.1	38.3	38.0
Japan:				
Nissan	n.a.	14.1	18.3	19.0
Honda	n.a.	10.1	19.1	22.1
Toyota	n.a.	13.6	17.3	19.6
Mazda	n.a.	13.3	17.3	n.a.
Germany:				
Daimler Benz	49.3	51.2	50.2	49.3
Volkswagen	n.a.	51.9	47.8	49.3
Ford Werke	46.0	44.4	35.0	n.a.
Opel	45.3	44.4	33.3	n.a.
BMW	45.7	49.8	46.2	46.4
United Kingdom:				
BLMC/Rover	33.6	29.5	32.1	28.8
Ford UK	n.a.	30.5	29.9	24.9
Talbot	n.a.	23.6	16.6	12.6
Vauxhall	n.a.	24.4	12.3	10.0
France:				
Renault	38.0	42.7	31.3	38.0
Peugeot PSA	n.a.	46.7	48.2	49.8
Peugeot	36.0	41.3	43.7	40.8
Citroen	n.a.	37.8	40.1	37.2
Italy:				
Fiat	n.a.	n.a.	49.5	51.1
Sweden:				
Volvo	n.a.	25.4	24.8	26.2

n.a.= not available

1. Vertical Integration = inverse of ratio of purchases to turnover.

Source: J.J. Chanaron (1988).

43

Despite its low degree of vertical integration, Japanese automobile and parts firms have a high degree of collaboration because of their unique structural relationship. Ofter termed ''kereitsu'', which refers to clusters of related companies organised under a loose umbrella structure, their relationship is characterised by informal networks, long-term contracts and joint product development. Japanese automakers often form associations or clubs to increase communications links with and between their auto parts suppliers and to reduce risks through intercorporate stockholding, financial ties and mutual assistance. Japanese automakers generally buy from few sources and maintain long-term contracts with suppliers, who may lower prices in exchange for larger profits over the longer run. Parts suppliers in Japan also play a large role in the design, development and continual improvement of parts through the life of the contract.

Auto parts procurement has been very different in the automoible industries of the United States and Europe. While they have a low ratio of dependence on outside orders, they tend to use many different subcontractors who do not belong to any organised system. Most automakers have short-term contracts with outside parts suppliers which they play off against one another to attain price advantages. US and European automobile manufacturers have also relied largely on their own resources for design and engineering of parts which suppliers make in accordance with automaker specifications.

Some analysts maintain that weaknesses in assembler-supplier relationships have been one reason the US and European automobile industries have lost market share to Japan. The interdependent relationships of the Japanese industry overcome many of the inefficiencies of the more rigid vertically-integrated model. The decentralisation of R&D and technology development in the Japanese system is said to increase innovation. The structural organisation of parts firms in Japan increases procurement efficiency. Japanese parts suppliers are concerned with maintaining high quality and lower costs and are highly responsive to demand trends and consumer preferences. Heavy reliance on outside parts suppliers has also helped Japanese automakers maintain high levels of productivity.

The structural relationship of Japanese automakers and parts suppliers also contributes to the difficulties encountered by foreign firms in selling original equipment and replacement parts for Japanese cars. The long-term contracts limit opportunities for outside suppliers. Many foreign firms do not sell the subassemblies or unit components purchased by Japanese automakers. Foreign auto parts firms may not have the necessary skills to engage in independent product engineering and cost reduction. They may have difficulties obtaining or interpreting the technical specifications of Japanese firms, which also leads to barriers in production of aftermarket parts.

American and European automakers have shown interest in the Japanese-style subcontracting system as a means of increasing competitiveness. Producers are reorganising their parts suppliers so they do not have to deal with an excessive number of companies, eliminating dual sourcing and encouraging mergers in the auto parts industry. Ford Europe is attempting to reduce the number of its suppliers from 2 500 to 900, Peugeot from 2 000 to 950, Renault from 1 415 to 900 and Austin-Rover from 1 200 to 700. US firms are entering into longer-term relationships with parts companies and relying on them more heavily for design and product improvements. General Motors recently announced plans to create a family of outside suppliers who would enjoy life-cycle procurement for parts for particular models and participate in design discussions from an early stage. Most of these concepts are being tried in General Motors' Saturn project to build a world competitive car in cost and quality.

C. Delivery

Delivery of auto parts to automobile manufacturers became a competitive factor in this industry with the advent of the Japanese just-in-time system. Japanese automakers require their suppliers to operate according to this process, which involves producing the exact parts needed, in the volume they are needed and delivering them to the plant when they are needed. Daily deliveries to assembly plants operate according to a synchronised system where parts are identified by bar codes indicating the model and reference number of the targeted vehicle, the point of delivery and the hour the vehicle will pass a specified assembly point. Some parts may be delivered only once a day, hourly deliveries may be made of parts such as seats or electrical systems, while parts such as headlights, glass products or batteries may be delivered every 2 to 4 hours.

This system calls for an expanded role for auto parts suppliers and their close attention to delivery times and quality. Because there are no back-up parts for replacing defective ones and because automakers do not generally inspect delivered parts, suppliers must work to eliminate defects during the production process. Technical competence, an emphasis on quality and a close working relationship with the automakers are required from the parts suppliers. In most cases, the just-in-time system also calls for the close geographic proximity of auto parts companies to automobile assembly sites.

The just-in-time system has competitive advantages in reducing the need for automakers and suppliers to maintain extensive inventories, quickly revealing defects and production bottlenecks, increasing flexibility in responding to market demand and decreasing inspection, storage and handling costs. Partly as a result of this system, Japanese automakers reduced the number of hours needed to build a car from 250 to about 140 in the early 1980s, compared with an average 200 hours in US and European plants. The just-in-time system also gives more responsibility for diagnosing problems, spotting defects and repairing equipment to line workers and reduces the need for supervisors, inspectors, repairmen and middle managers. Japanese automakers have been able to reduce employment at several levels and achieve marked increases in labour productivity.

US and European firms generally hold large stocks or inventories of parts throughout the automobile plant in an effort to achieve the longest possible production runs and to ensure against equipment breakdowns, labour strikes, defective parts and interruptions in parts supply. Automakers also check parts which reduces the pressure on suppliers to deliver defect-free components and lowers their initial costs. Recognising the economies and efficiencies of the just-in-time system, many US and European firms are now implementing these techniques and trying to improve the efficiency of their inventory management. Ford and General Motors are urging key suppliers in Europe to set up satellite production facilities close to assembly plants in an attempt to halve inventories and improve efficiency. As more OECD automakers adopt Japanese-style delivery systems, they are demanding improved quality and performance from auto parts suppliers.

D. Quality

The quality image and reliability of their automobiles is considered one of the reasons for the competitive success of Japanese automakers in other OECD countries. Increased competition in OECD markets has prompted all automakers to give more attention to the quality of auto parts and to place more of this responsibility on the parts suppliers. More widespread use of just-in-time delivery systems has also prompted a greater focus on product quality.

Japanese automobile companies enjoy a continuing reputation for high-quality products. Consumer groups in the United States have consistently rated Japanese cars high in terms of quality and reliability and give particularly good ratings to individual parts such as engines, brakes and clutches. The International Motor Vehicle Programme (IMVP), centred at the Massachusetts Institute of Technology, recently concluded that Japanese automobile quality is still superior to other producers and that US automakers are catching up more rapidly than European firms. In one IMVP study, Japanese automobiles sold in the United States were found to average 44 assembly defects per 100 compared to 87 for US cars and 90 for European cars.

Most credit for the quality image of Japanese automobiles is due to the auto parts suppliers, who have the ultimate responsibility for controls, standards and guarantees. Quality controls for parts are stringent; rejection rates are less than 1 per 1 000 parts and closer to 1 per 10 000 parts delivered. Japanese auto parts suppliers practice Total Quality Control in their shops testing 100 per cent of parts under real functioning conditions. High quality standards are due to extensive factory automation and management techniques such as quality circles. The performance of Japanese parts suppliers is also explained by a sustained effort of tangible and intangible investment which could be undertaken in a sheltered domestic market. The responsibility of Japanese parts suppliers for guarantees does not cease with delivery of the part but extends to the auto purchaser's guarantee. US and European automakers are increasingly following the Japanese example in choosing their main parts suppliers on the basis of their capacity to respect and guarantee strict standards of quality.

E. Costs and Prices

Auto parts suppliers compete on the basis of price as well as delivery and quality. Intensified competition in the automobile industry has led producers to squeeze their suppliers on prices and to attempt to make them more cost-competitive. American and European automakers, in particular, have tried to take better control of the factors determining production costs including parts supply. They are urging increased investment and efficiency on the part of their inhouse suppliers and encouraging other suppliers to seek joint ventures with Japanese firms. Even Nissan and Toyota have recently developed a multi-sourcing system to encourage competition among parts suppliers to reduce prices. In response, many auto parts firms are diversifying their clients for original equipment parts and seeking greater sales in the more profitable replacement market.

Auto parts suppliers have also had to adapt to the shortening of standard model life cycles from 10 years to 4 years. Competition is pushing this gap between new car models to three years. Japanese automakers are introducing full model changes once every four years and minor changes at shorter intervals to make their products more marketable. Between 1980 and 1984, Japanese firms introduced 15 new standard small car models while US firms brought out 3. Due to the rapidity of standard model changes, auto parts suppliers must be able to make profound product and process changes at low cost in a short amount of time. The standard model life of only four years has also reduced the merits of large volume production for parts producers.

The increasing diversity of automobile models has been another cost pressure on parts suppliers. Most automakers are attempting to supply a full line of models and versions in order to meet the many commercial and technological niches into which car markets are now fragmented. In response to Japanese competition, all automakers are pushing production volumes lower and offering a much wider range of models with a greater variety of options. For example, the number of distinct European models on offer in the economy range doubled from 30 in 1970 to more than 60 in the early 1980s. This is made possible by the increasing use of platforms, which allow modified versions of cars for different segments of the market. Auto parts suppliers must be able to produce many variations on standard parts and to adjust rapidly to changing specifications without price penalties.

F.   Technology

Technology is becoming a more important factor in the competitiveness of the auto parts industry due to the growing technological contribution to automobile value and the decentralisation of technical responsibilities. Because cars of the 1990s will incorporate a whole range of new technologies offering improved performance, fuel economy, emission control and safety and comfort, product technology may be the future competitive battleground in auto parts production and trade.

The fastest growing component of automobiles in terms of value-added are electronics systems. Some forecast that by the year 2000, electronics will account for 24 percent of the manufacturing cost of the average car compared with 5 per cent at present. Future markets are estimated as high as $60 billion (see Table 14). The "intelligent car" of the future will include sensors and electronics for engine management, anti-lock brakes, door locks, on-board diagnostics, climate control and digital displays. Electronic systems for steering, braking and accelerating may be integrated under the control of on-board computers. Large auto parts suppliers are now linking up with electronics firms to develop these high value-added components: Allied Signal and Siemens, Bosch and Intel, AEG and Alcatel. One of the first electronic car component manufacturing ventures, that of Ford in Spain, is expected to be at full capacity in 1993 producing electronic control modules to manage critical aspects of vehicle performance.

New materials are the other technological revolution in automobiles; some forecast that by the year 2000, 20 to 30 per cent of the weight of the average car may be made up of plastic composites and other advanced materials compared to less than 8 per cent at present. Although it was previously thought that composites could not supplant metals in the key stress-bearing parts of a vehicle, research has shown that new materials can provide strength and lightness at a

Table 14.   **Forecasts of Automotive Electronics Markets**

US$ million

	United States	Japan	Europe
1985	5 000	4 000	2 000
1990	11 000	11 000	7 000
1995	14 000	15 000	15 000
2000	19 000	19 000	21 000

Source: J.J. Chanaron (1988).

production cost competitive with that of steel. General Motors plans production of a minivan in 1989 constructed of an aluminum cage covered with composite plastic panels. Many OECD chemical companies as well as the larger auto parts firms are developing composite technology, while intense research continues on ceramic engines and engine parts. The three large US automakers – General Motors, Ford and Chrysler – have formed a consortium for joint research on automotive applications for plastic composites, including structural components.

Responsibility for the development of new technologies and their incorporation into products is gradually shifting from the automakers to the auto parts suppliers. US and European automakers were traditionally responsible for the technical concepts of auto design, while parts suppliers were tasked with the execution of these concepts. Japanese rethinking of the organisation of automobile production gave parts suppliers more responsibility for the technical and design functions. While automakers in all countries still conduct a large share of research and development, parts firms are taking more initiative for technological development and are more closely involved in model improvements and innovations.

The larger auto parts firms are expanding their engineering, design and research and development capabilities in line with their growing technical responbilities. A survey of 92 American auto parts suppliers showed they placed emphasis on improving their R&D capacity second only to improving quality as a means of increasing their competitiveness. However, most SMEs don't have the financial or human resources needed for an autonomous R&D capability. Auto parts research in Japan is conducted by the first tier component manufacturers, who have maintained R&D as a share of turnover at an average 2.5 per cent in the 1980s increasing to 3.5 per cent in 1986. Outside of the largest multinationals, most US and European auto parts firms have not reached this level of research intensity. Japanese parts makers are beginning to reap the benefits of their previous investments in R&D and are considered as advanced in technology as the best firms in Europe and North America.

IV. INDUSTRIAL AND TRADE POLICIES

A. United States

The United States government, like that of most other OECD countries, has had no specific industrial policies for the automotive parts sector, which has benefited indirectly from aids to the automobile industry. The auto parts sector has also benefited from horizontal policies – R&D, fiscal, regional and SME – and other programmes aimed at improving the environment for all manufacturing sectors. As the US automotive parts sector faces growing foreign competition in the domestic market, the government may receive increasing demands for direct or indirect assistance in restructuring and technology development.

The increasing trade deficit with Japan in both automobiles and automotive parts prompted the US Government in the early 1980s to consider trade policy approaches to redress the imbalance. Since May 1981, automobile exports from Japan to the United States have been reduced, initially through bilaterally-agreed voluntary export restraints. This has provided US automakers a period of time to improve competitiveness through product improvements and other adjustments and also maintained demand levels for the automotive parts industry. In May 1986, the United States and Japan added transportation machinery to the Market Oriented Sector Selective (MOSS) talks, which provided a forum for discussing ways to expand access to the Japanese auto parts market. The talks resulted in the initiation of a data collection system to monitor US auto parts sales to Japanese automakers, the establishment of a US Auto Parts Industry office in Japan and other steps for facilitating contacts between US auto parts suppliers and potential Japanese customers.

The US Government has also provided assistance to the auto parts industry under the Trade Adjustment Assistance programme, which assists employees in situations where imports have been a significant contributor to job losses. Between 1982 and 1987, the government approved assistance to over 380 000 workers from various auto parts subsectors, including tires and rubber products, body parts and stampings, electrical equipment and carburetors, piston rings and valves. The government provided financial and technical assistance to some 16 auto parts firms under the TAA programme in this period. Also under the TAA programme, the US Department of Commerce and the US Motor and Equipment Manufacturers Association established an auto parts industry office in Japan.

At the state and local government level, a variety of investment incentives have been offered to both domestic and foreign automotive parts firms. Loans, grants, tax abatements, training funds and assistance for building and development costs are among the incentives available to companies willing to open production facilities and provide employment in specific areas. Although domestic auto parts firms have received the greatest share of these incentives, foreign investors have been increasing their portion in recent years. Table 15 shows the

Table 15. **Geographic Distribution of Japanese Auto Parts Firms in the United States**

Percentages

State	Share	State	Share
Michigan	26.3	Illinois	6.9
Ohio	13.5	Pennsylvania	3.6
Tennessee	12.0	California	3.6
Kentucky	9.9	Other	14.6
Indiana	9.6		
		Total	100.0

Source: Ward's Auto World.

geographic distribution of Japanese automotive parts firms in the United States, which largely reflects the location of automobile assembly facilities as well as the availability of investment incentives in some states.

B. Japan

Japanese Government approaches to industrial restructuring, technology development and market protection, particularly in the 1960s and 1970s, benefited both the automobile industry and parts suppliers. The Japanese Government, somewhat unsuccessfuly, originally sought to develop large independent components firms as a means of aiding the automotive industry; at the same time, it attempted to merge the domestic automobile companies into three larger groups. In the absence of this restructuring, the keiretsu structure of the industry has provided a ready-made network for the distribution of information, technology diffusion and policy development. As the Japanese auto parts industry may need further rationalisation in view of the number of financially weak SMEs, industry policies may turn to restructuring both the industry and its internal markets in light of increasing trade imbalances and frictions, growing foreign investment and declining domestic automobile assembly.

Japan's foreign competitors complain of closed domestic markets and non-tariff barriers to the imports of automotive parts. Prior to the 1970s, both the automble and auto parts sectors were shielded from foreign competition by import quotas and tariffs, restrictions on inward investment and strict licensing provisions. Despite the removal of these constraints, foreign auto parts suppliers have had little success in the Japanese market partly due to Japanese business and commercial practices. Close consumer-supplier relationships, complex distributions systems and long-term contracts are among the factors contributing to low import penetration in the auto parts sector.

Both the United States and the EEC continue to seek market openings in Japan for their auto parts suppliers. The United States has refused to lift sanctions on Japanese electronics imports in part because of the failure of Japan's auto parts industry to increase sufficiently purchases of US semiconductors. The Japanese Government, largely as a result of the MOSS talks with the United States, undertook a campaign to ensure that the government vehicle inspection programme does not disciminate against automobiles with foreign parts and is taking other steps to encourage increased purchases of foreign parts by its motor vehicle industry. As a result of the MOSS talks, the Governments of Japan and the United States are cooperating in providing up-to-date contact lists of Japanese motor vehicle manufacturers for Japan and US facilities and in developing seminars to acquaint US parts manufacturers with techniques for obtaining business opportunities with Japanese companies.

C.   Europe

Although the European countries have not had specific industrial policies for the auto parts sector at either the national or EEC level, governments have given incentives and assistance for industry restructuring. The French Government has given assistance to its auto parts sector through IDICA, the branch of the Institut de Developpement Industriel specialising in auto components. Valeo, the large French auto parts firms, was recently directed by the EEC to repay interest subsidies received on state loans from 1986. The French, Italian and German Governments have in the past played a role in rationalising their components industries and blocked cross-national mergers they deemed detrimental to domestic interests. In the United Kingdom, where the components industry has experienced a shakeout through the operation of market forces, the British Chamber of Commerce is calling for government intervention to assist the industry in restructuring and technology development.

The European countries are now showing a greater willingness to seek cross-national solutions to improving the competitiveness of the auto parts industry. Major barriers to intra-EEC trade in automobiles and parts include the lack of a single approval and certification system, differing exhaust emission standards, national vehicle equipment requirements and different taxation levels on automobile sales. An EEC-wide approval system is proposed for all automotive components, including windshields and tires. A more uniform value-added tax is proposed to replace VAT rates ranging from 12 per cent in Luxembourg to 33 per cent in Spain.

The EEC currently supports collaborative industry research on automotive parts as part of the Eureka programme. In the Prometheus project, 13 European automakers are undertaking joint research to develop automotive electronics systems to improve vehicle safety and moderate adverse environmental effects. In the Carmat project, European automobile, chemical and other companies are researching new materials for automotive parts focusing on plastic composites, ceramics and reinforced metals.

As in the United States, European actions to limit automobile imports from Japan have reduced competitive pressures on the automotive parts sector. At present, Japanese auto imports account for less than 1 per cent of the Italian and Spanish markets, for about 3 per cent of the French market and for 11 per cent of the UK market. Local content requirements for foreign automobile assembly plants have been implemented by some European countries as well as the granting of investment incentives. The United Kingdom gave investment incentives to construction of a Ford engine plant and to the siting of the Nissan assembly facility. Austria has given assistance for the construction of a General Motors engine plant. Spain has provided incentives to Ford for its new electronics component facility and to General Electric for plastics components production.

D.   Other OECD

The Canadian auto parts industry, located primarily in Ontario, accounts for about 12 per cent of the joint Canadian and US market. Canadian automotive production capacity (vehicles and parts) is the sixth largest in the world. About 20 per cent of the auto parts industry is Canadian-owned; Canada's principal automotive parts manufacturers, with the exception of Magna International, are subsidiaries of US and European firms. The Federal Government has not played a large role in the development of this sector. However, the Government of Ontario has given some emphasis to the development of the auto parts industry; through the Ontario Centre for Automotive Parts Technology, which is now in the private sector, it has provided technical and financial assistance to over 700 firms and 10 000 persons-days of technical training.

The US-Canada Automotive Products Trade Agreement (Auto Pact) of 1965 essentially provides for duty-free treatment of trade between the two parties in eligible auto parts used as original equipment in the manufacture of automobiles. Canada permits auto pact members to import auto parts duty free on a multilateral basis. The Canada-US Free Trade Agreement (FTA) was implemented commencing January 1, 1989 and reconfirms the Auto Pact. The agreement also provides for a new, more stringent rule of origin which, in the case of the automotive sector, will serve to increase domestic sourcing in North America. The rule of origin under the FTA is based on North American value assessed on eligible processing and material costs and not on national content level, which usually includes profits, administrative costs and a range of other costs.

Australia's automotive parts industry is a major part of the manufacturing sector and supplies the local automotive manufacturers Nissan, Toyota, Ford, Holden and Mitsubishi, and a growing export market. This export market in 1987 was valued at US$433 million and included such countries as Germany, Japan and Korea. Australia is currently running a small trade deficit of about US$300 million in automotive parts, mostly due to imports of components from Japan. Manufacturers are allowed to import up to 15 per cent of their components duty-free. In April 1988, the Australian Government announced changes to the Passenger Motor Vehicle Plan aimed at continuing the process of structural change in the automobile industry and continuing improved performance in the components sector. These changes consisted of eliminating quotas, reducing tariffs and reducing penalties for non-compliance with the 85 per cent local content target. Exports of automotive parts are to be further encouraged through increasing the upper limit of export credits and providing additional credits for superior export performance.

E.   Non-OECD Countries

Although some 46 developing countries currently host production or assembly of automobiles by OECD firms, only five or six are considered major automobile producers based on an average local parts content of more than 50 to 60 per cent. These are Korea, Brazil, Mexico, Argentina, India and possibly Taiwan. OECD firms established automobile production facilities in many NIEs to meet local demand and were often required to achieve a specified local parts content. Automotive parts sectors in the NIEs, which now account for about 2 per cent of world production, are largely locally-owned and produce smaller components at low scales of output. Government policies are gradually shifting from a high degree of protection to encouraging more technology transfer from the OECD countries and a greater degree of global interaction.

Korea is the only NIE to develop a truly indigenous automobile industry, with over 87 per cent of components for its assemblers supplied locally by Korean firms. The government adopted a policy of building a local parts industry on the basis of licensing and other interfirm arrangements with foreign companies rather than on the basis of direct investment. Between 1980 and 1986, Korean automotive parts firms entered into 21 joint ventures and 160 technology licensing agreements with OECD auto parts companies, about 60 per cent of the latter with Japanese firms. The government also gave investment assistance to firms producing larger components such as engines, transmissions and axles. The Korea Auto Industries Cooperative Association (KAICA) now has over 900 members of which 70 per cent are SMEs with less than 50 employees. Most firms still produce on a small scale, import about 20 per cent of their basic materials and rely heavily on foreign partners for technology. However, Korea has started exporting about 10 per cent of its auto parts production, mostly to Japan. The Korean Government is attempting to strengthen research and development in the auto parts sector and to retructure the industry to promote greater specialisation, economies of scale and quality improvements.

Taiwan established an automotive local content level in 1980 with the aim of developing a largely self-sufficient automobile industry by the 1990s. The government provides tax exemptions and other financial benefits to companies meeting local content levels, now approaching 50 to 60 per cent. Duties on imported automotive parts and components start at 45 per cent and are over 80 per cent for automobiles. Like Korea, Taiwan prohibits imports of automobiles from Japan. To circumvent these restrictions, Honda is now exporting automobiles produced in the United States to both Taiwan and Korea.

Recurrent attempts have been made to develop a local automotive components industry through an Association of Southeast Asian Nations (Asean) Car. The Asean countries reached an agreement in October 1988 to produce automobiles using regionally manufactured components with the help of Japan's Mitsubishi. Import duties on automotive parts shipped between participating countries will be reduced. Thailand is expected to produce windshields and metal molds, Malaysia will produce door panels and other body parts and the Philippines will supply transmission parts and frames for trucks. In addition to plans for the Asean car, Mitsubishi is currently producing automobiles in Thailand for export to North America, Malaysia is promoting its national car, the Proton Saga, and Indonesia is aiming for complete local automobile production by 1992.

In Latin America, Brazil and Mexico are the main locales for offshore auto parts production by OECD firms, mostly US companies who supply components to auto assemblers and increasingly export parts back to the United States. Brazil is the largest automobile producer among the NIEs with a local content level averaging over 80 per cent. After Brazil and Korea, Mexico has the third highest level of automobile output and a local content average of 60 to 70 per cent. US firms have established engine production facilities in Mexico, which is now estimated to have an engine production capacity of over 2 million units per year, and Mexico's duty-free zones are attracting increasing US and Japanese investment in auto parts production. Argentina, whose local content is well over 80 per cent, has had declining vehicle production in the last ten years. Latin American governments have maintained tariffs on imports of automotive parts, offered incentives to exports and often coupled local content mandates with other performance requirements. Export performance requirements are now being emphasized more than local content rules, which have been relaxed in Brazil and Mexico.

V. MAJOR ISSUES

A. Global Firm Strategies and Industrial Policies

The internationalisation of auto parts activities in terms of trade and investment may call for new firm strategies and government policy approaches. Prior to the l980s, trade in auto parts was limited and largely intra-firm. Foreign investment was mostly by US companies. OECD auto parts sectors were relatively isolated from foreign competition. Technological trends are leading to more international markets and possibly a return to the global car concept, adding to international competition in the auto parts industry.

As the large automakers source more parts from domestic and foreign suppliers on the basis of technology, quality and cost, the internationalisation of parts suppliers will continue to grow. US and European automakers are moving away from vertical integration and towards the Japanese ratio of 80 per cent external purchases. It is forecast that the percentage of foreign parts in cars produced by US automakers will increase from 10 per cent at present to 17 per cent in the early l990s. General Motors is building components facilities in Japan to supply parts to its US plants, while Japanese auto parts firms in North America are starting to export to Europe and to assemblers in Japan.

As more original equipment parts are purchased from foreign suppliers in the OECD countries, competition in the aftermarket will also intensify. More Japanese and European firms are competing in the market for replacement parts for autos built by US firms, while US and Japanese firms are supplying the aftermarket for European car parts. In North America, the fastest-growing segment of the aftermarket is that for replacement parts for Japanese vehicles, which now account for 15 per cent of the US registered car fleet. However this market remains difficult to penetrate. Only recently have US parts firms starting producing components for Japanese cars, which involves a relatively large investment and a departure from traditional product lines. The aftermarket for Japanese car parts is also growing in Europe; Nissan recently located its European parts centre in Amsterdam, where it claims to have the most technologically advanced delivery system for replacement parts and services in Europe.

Growing foreign investment in automotive parts will continue to prompt structural change in this sector. The acceleration of the movement of Japanese and European auto parts firms to North America since l985 is partly due to the depreciation of the dollar. The appreciation of the yen has also prompted Japanese firms to plan more investments in European locales. Japanese automobile manufacturers abroad have encouraged relocation by their suppliers to offset penalties associated with components produced in yen and shipped from Japan. Another major stimulant to foreign investment has been fear of increasing trade and investment restrictions, including local content requirements for automobiles. As more Japanese automakers build assembly plants abroad, it is predicted that almost 20 per cent of Japan's auto parts production will also be overseas by the mid-l990s.

Some believe that changes in automobile design and technology will prompt a return to the concept of a global car. The initial attempts to produce world cars at the end of the 1970s – General Motor's J-car and Ford's Escort – were a partial failure in that many changes were needed to adapt the vehicles to individual markets. However, it did allow US producers to set up large-scale production of some core components for use worldwide. The increasing use of platforms in automobile production and the evolution of parts suppliers into systems suppliers may lead again to a common range of cars to be built worldwide. Some studies predict a reduction in the number of standard platforms, increases in production per platform and greater specialisation in components. More responsibility will be placed on auto parts firms both to supply systems and subassemblies to automakers and to vary these for consumer tastes. The larger, technologically-advanced components firms who can become part of these worldwide production systems will benefit. The former notion of international specialisation of production units is now being undermined by "just-in-time," which is based on the geographic proximity of manufacturers and parts suppliers and which permits the development of flexible workshops.

Due to growing international competition, firm strategies in the auto parts sector must be focused on achieving advantages in key areas: flexibility and timeliness in delivery and assembly; quality in production through new management and technical systems; technological excellence through research and development; economies of scale supporting greater product differentiation through restructuring; and global positioning through foreign investment and strategic alliances with foreign firms. It should be mentioned that small- and medium-sized enterprises may encounter special difficulties in developing competitive strategies although they also may have opportunities in the production of smaller scale products for niche markets. Although any new global strategies should be adopted in response to market developments, auto parts sectors may look to governments for assistance in interim restructuring, technology development and improving competitiveness. OECD governments may need to review industrial policy approaches which can contribute to adjustment in this sector, prevent the development of trade imbalances and obviate the need for restrictive trade and/or investment practices. In general, government policies should avoid emphasizing national champions in the auto parts sector and promote interfirm cooperation and overall competitiveness.

B. Local Content Rules

One of the most contentious trade issues in the automotive parts sector relates to national policies requiring or encouraging a level of local parts content for automobiles produced domestically. Local content is the sum of the value of parts and materials procured from domestic sources plus the value of domestic assembly labour, overhead and markups. Another term, local or domestic sourcing, refers only to the value of parts and materials procured domestically in relation to the total value of components used to manufacture a car. Policies setting levels of local content or local sourcing have become more widespread as foreign investment in automobile assembly and associated trade in auto parts has increased.

Local content rules for automobiles are generally intended to foster the development of domestic automotive parts producers through import substitution. Non-OECD countries wishing to develop auto parts industries have long had policies on local content, although these have been softened in recent years in an effort to decrease inefficiencies and increase exports. Brazil imposed local content requirements on its motor vehicle industry starting in 1956. Mexico's local content requirements were put in place in 1962 and Korea's in 1966. Most OECD countries do not have mandatory local content requirements for automobile manufacture, but may negotiate commitments from foreign assemblers for certain levels of local content in return for government financial assistance or other benefits. Australia has a local content target of 85 per cent for automobile manufacturers, and the United States and Canada negotiated a 50 per cent North American value provision as the preference rule for tariff treatment under the Canada-US Free Trade Agreement. It applies to all automotive trade not already covered by the Auto Pact of 1965.

Although the United States has no local content legislation, protectionist sentiments have grown with foreign investment in US assembly facilities and rising parts imports. Japanese automobile firms have opened or have under construction 10 North American automobile assembly plants, and the Korean firm Hyundai is opening a facility in Canada (see Table 16). Japanese automakers forecast capacity to build 2.2 million vehicles per year in the United States and Canada by 1990. The initial plants opened with about 30 per cent local content increasing to 50 to 60 per cent in 1988. Most companies have announced their intention to achieve 75 per cent North American value added by the early 1990s. Local parts content is growing due to the relocation of Japanese parts firms to North America and the increasing number of US and Canadian companies able to meet the quality and delivery expectations of Japanese automakers.

Plans for increased Japanese automobile assembly capacity in Europe have led to controversy over local content levels and calls for a European local content policy. Nissan, which now has the only Japanese automobile assembly facility in Europe, pledged to increase local content from 60 per cent to 80 per cent by 1991. Nissan also produces commercial vehicles in Spain, and the Austin Rover group makes Honda automobiles in the United Kingdom. Toyota, Mitsubishi, Subaru, Suzuki and other Japanese firms are studying the feasibility of establishing assembly plants in Europe. One EEC study predicts that between 500 000 and 800 000 vehicles will be assembled annually in Japanese plants in Europe by the 1990s.

Table 16. **North American Value by Foreign Plant**

Location	Company	Start-up (year)	Capacity (units)	Employees	N. American Value (%)	
					1988	1990
US	Honda	1982	360 000	4 200	60	75
	Nissan	1983	260 000	3 300	60	80
	Toyota/GM	1984	250 000	2 500	60	75
	Mazda	1987	240 000	3 500	50	70
	Toyota	1988	200 000	3 000	60	70
	MMC/Chrys	1988	240 000	2 900	60	60
	Fuji/Isuzu	1989	60 000	1 700		50
Canada	Honda	1986	120 000	1 200	40	50
	Toyota	1988	50 000	1 000	50	50
	Suzuki/GM	1989	200 000	2 000		50
	Hyundai	1989	100 000	1 350		50

Source: Adapted from national sources.

Recent local content disputes have stemmed from exports of automobiles from Nissan's plant in England to France and Italy. In general, the problem is not so much legal as strategic: Japanese firms will need to attain a local content level of more than 80 per cent if they wish to be significant actors in the European market. Like Ford and General Motors, they need to be integrated at the economic and social levels in order to follow real trends in specific markets.

In general, international rules on local content and on determining the origin of a product are ill-defined. Yet local content policies may continue to be used owing to growth in foreign investment and the rising importance of high-technology industries which draw on a multiplicity of parts sources. The General Agreement on Tariffs and Trade (GATT) has no specific provisions to define whether and under what conditions local content requirements can be used as instruments of trade policy, although they are being discussed in the Uruguay Round talks on Trade Related Investment Measures (TRIMs). Many believe that local content policies constitute unfair trade restrictions and that their use should be regulated under the GATT. Other countries, including many developing countries, maintain that such policies help channel investment to particular sectors. Local content policies in the auto parts sector are intended to realize the full positive effects of foreign investment on local economies and have developed in response to changing relationships between manufacturers and parts suppliers. However, governments need to agree on rules for the use of these measures in the GATT.

C. Foreign Investment Issues

In the 1980s, there has been a shift in the industrial and trade policies of several OECD countries from a focus on automobile assemblers towards a joint focus on assembly and automotive parts production. This policy shift was largely spurred by changing foreign investment patterns, particularly increasing investment by Japanese automobile manufacturers and auto parts producers in other OECD areas. Automobile and automotive parts production forecasts to the 1990s show that the domestic Japanese share of world output is expected to decline, while the US and European share will grow largely due to foreign investment. These trends have raised concerns regarding the effects of foreign investment on competitiveness, employment, production capacity and technology development in host countries. They have also raised policy questions regarding Government incentives and disincentives to foreign investment in automotive parts.

Auto parts firms in both North America and Europe fear they will lose domestic market share to foreign suppliers, particularly Japanese parts firms, as the Japanese share of their automobile markets increases and as Japanese firms supply parts to other automakers. Japanese parts manufacturers equal or surpass other OECD industries in most competitiveness measures, including quality, delivery, design and price. However, foreign investment is prompting North American auto parts firms to improve their overall competitive posture. US auto parts companies are adopting Japanese production techniques and can now match the productivity of Japanese assemblers and very nearly equal the quality of Japanese auto parts. Increased foreign investment could also spur European parts makers to improve the quality of their products and manufacturing efficiency. Foreign investment can generate the pressure needed to ensure that the auto parts industry remains globally competitive rather than dependent on narrow domestic markets. It can also promote needed restructuring in the parts sector, which in most OECD countries includes a large segment of small, inefficient producers.

Another concern is the effect of foreign investment on auto parts employment. In North America, some fear that the operations of Japanese auto assemblers and parts firms will result in job losses because they use fewer workers and more foreign content than US automakers. A United Auto Workers (UAW) study in 1986 estimated that there would be 200 000 fewer US auto-related jobs in 1990 due to investment by Japanese automakers. US Government studies predict that US auto-related employment may be smaller by some 45 000 jobs in 1990; this would be due not only to overall gains in worker productivity, but also to increased use of foreign parts by US automakers as well as to imports by Japanese automakers. Jidoshasoren, the Japanese automobile trade union, is predicting that 75 000 auto-related jobs in Japan will disappear by 1990 due to foreign investment which substitutes for Japanese exports. Employment levels associated with foreign investment will largely depend on the extent to which Japanese firms displace the production of other OECD producers or imports of parts from Japan.

The OECD automobile industry is also worried about the danger of overcapacity in both automobile assembly and parts production as a result of high levels of foreign investment. Because such investment is often intended to surmount trade barriers rather than supply expected demand, it may not be fully responsive to global demand trends. At present, there are predictions of excess capacity of 2 to 3 million vehicles in the North American automobile market in the early 1990s. If all Japanese auto investment plans are carried out, there are also forecasts of overcapacity in the European market. Although some believe that the threat of overcapacity due to foreign investment is exaggerated, most observers forecast some degree of global overcapacity in automobile and parts production by the 1990s.

The technological content of foreign investment is also controversial. Host countries fear that investors will transfer low value-added operations abroad and keep high value-added activities such as research and development and manufacture of high technology components at home. Until recently, Japanese automakers in North America have purchased most bulky low-technology components such as carpets, plastic assemblies, glass and tires from local parts makers and imported high-value added parts and assemblies – engines, transaxles, suspension and brakes. However, Japanese parts firms are now investing in engine production and other high value-added activities abroad. Japanese automakers have found that the need to customise products for local markets requires resident design and engineering staff. Both Japanese assemblers and parts makers are now developing their R&D capabilities in North America to produce regional versions of basic products by the early 1990s. Japanese firms are also giving technical assistance to US and European parts makers through joint venture and other interfirm arrangements.

It is generally believed that foreign investment in auto parts in the OECD area can stimulate competitiveness and technology development in the industry although substantial restructuring may be needed. However, the positive effects of foreign investment may not be fully realised without greater attempts by Japanese automakers to integrate foreign parts firms into their supply networks at an early stage in vehicle development. Other OECD firms have captured only a fraction of the parts market in Japan, often supplying components for vehicles destined for export to their own markets. The close assembler-supplier relationships of the Japanese automobile industry are among the business practices limiting foreign access to the Japanese market in Japan as well as in North America and Europe. Lack of experience fabricating OE parts contributes to the difficulties of foreign firms in the aftermarket for Japanese parts. OECD trade and investment frictions in the automotive parts sector could be partly resolved through a more comprehensive opening of the Japanese auto parts market at home and abroad.

OECD governments are using financial and other incentives to attract foreign investment in automotive parts primarily to generate development and employment. In this way, the United

States, Canada and many European countries continue to attract Japanese and other foreign investors in automobile and parts production. At the same time, concern is appearing about the effects of foreign investment and associated imports on the competitiveness of indigenous parts producers. This has led to the use of local content requirements and proposals for implementing other types of controls on inward direct investment. OECD governments need to consider the full impacts of the use of such investment measures on promoting fair competition in automotive parts and restructuring in this sector.

REFERENCES

Chanaron, J.J. (1988), "L'industrie des pièces automobiles des pays de l'OCDE: Situation et perspectives", a report prepared in the context of the OECD Industry Division project on Internationalisation and Industrial Activities, October.

Commission of the European Communities (1988), *Panorama of EC Industry: 1989,* Luxembourg.

Des Rosiers, D. (1987), "The Size, Structure and Performance of the Canadian Automotive Parts Industry: Identifying Critical Success Factors", International Motor Vehicle Program.

Ikeda, Masayoshi (1987), "An International Comparison of Subcontracting Systems in the Automotive Component Manufacturing Industry", International Motor Vehicle Program.

Jo, Sung-Hwan (1988), *The Car Industry in the Republic of Korea,* World Employment Programme Research, International Labour Office, Geneva.

Lamming, R. (1987), "The International Automotive Components Industry", International Motor Vehicle Program.

U.S. Department of Commerce (1987), "Final Report on the MOSS Talks on Transportation Machinery," Washington, D.C., August.

U.S. General Accounting Office (1988), *Foreign Investment: Growing Japanese Presence in the U.S. Auto Industry,* Washington, D.C., March.

U.S. International Trade Commission (1987), *U.S. Global Competitiveness: The U.S. Automotive Parts Industry,* Washington, D.C., December.

THE CHEMICALS INDUSTRY

I. SUMMARY

The OECD chemicals industry – here confined to industrial chemicals, agricultural chemicals and pharmaceuticals – contributes 10 per cent of the value of manufacturing production and makes products used in a wide variety of sectors. The OECD countries account for over 75 per cent of world output of these chemicals. The European countries as a whole are the largest producers and exporters of chemicals and maintain a substantial trade surplus with the rest of the world. The United States accounts for a third of OECD chemicals production, but its market share and trade surplus are shrinking in the 1980s, particularly in pharmaceuticals. Japan's chemicals industry, which is not as highly developed or diversified as the US and European industries, has only recently increased exports and activities in foreign markets. About 70 per cent of OECD trade in chemicals is with other OECD countries; foreign investment in chemicals is growing and is extensive in the pharmaceuticals sector.

Competition in pharmaceuticals and many agricultural chemicals is based largely on product innovation while competition in most industrial chemicals is based on price. Highly research-intensive industries such as pharmaceuticals and agricultural chemicals depend on patents to earn adequate returns from their R&D expenditures. Several factors are eroding the returns to chemicals patents in the 1980s, including increased R&D costs, testing and registration delays which reduce the term of patent protection, generic products which have a growing share of the prescription drug market, and patent infringement by companies which illegally imitate and market patented chemicals products. Differences in national patent systems cause difficulties to chemicals firms operating internationally and reduce the economic returns to their patents and patent licenses.

The following are the major policy issues identified:

a) *Economic Costs of Patent Infringement:* It is estimated that the OECD chemicals industry – primarily producers of pharmaceuticals, plant protection chemicals and fertilizers – suffers annual economic losses of $7-$8 billion due to patent infringement. Economic costs to all OECD industries due to unauthorised use of intellectual property has been estimated at $70 billion or 3 per cent of the value of world merchandise trade.

b) *R&D Effects of Patent Infringement:* The chemicals industry is among those industrial sectors to which patent protection is vital in promoting the development and commercial introduction of new products. Increasing patent infringement may discourage the high rate of investment needed in research and development in chemicals, which is one of the key innovative sectors in OECD economies.

c) *Intellectual Property Rights and Industrial Policy:* Intellectual property rights can be used as instruments of industrial policy to stimulate technological progress and industrial development as well as to influence trade and foreign investment flows. Talks are being conducted in WIPO (World Intellectual Property Organisation) on harmonising international patent laws and in the GATT on trade-related aspects of intellectual property rights. OECD countries need to work within a multilateral framework towards a strengthened intellectual property rights system which is in the economic interest of all nations.

II. INDUSTRY BACKGROUND

A. Product Structure

This study reviews three main components of the chemicals industry - industrial chemicals, agricultural chemicals and pharmaceuticals - which account for the major share of the value of chemicals output in the OECD countries. Other miscellaneous components of the chemicals industry - e.g., rubber and plastics, coatings and adhesives, soaps and cosmetics -are not reviewed here.

Output of industrial chemicals is the largest of the three chemicals sectors (industrial chemicals, agricultural chemicals and pharmaceuticals) considered in this paper (see Table 17). Most industrial chemicals are basic chemicals used in the production of other chemical products. They are also termed heavy, bulk or commodity chemicals and are generally produced in larger volumes and earn smaller profit margins than agricultural chemicals or pharmaceuticals. Industrial chemicals can be divided into two main groups: organic chemicals which account for about 70 per cent of output value and inorganic chemicals which account for the remaining 30 per cent. Organic chemicals are generally based on petroleum and natural gas and include ethylene, propylene, methanol and their derivatives. Inorganic chemicals include chloralkalies, industrial gases, acids and salts.

Agricultural chemicals account for about 12 per cent of OECD output of the three chemicals sectors (industrial chemicals, agricultural chemicals and pharmaceuticals) considered in this paper. Agricultural chemicals can be divided into two main groups: nitrogenous and phosphatic fertilizers which account for 60 per cent of output value and pesticides which account for 40 per cent. In the pesticides group, herbicides account for roughly half of total sales, insecticides for 25 per cent and fungicides and growth regulators for the remainder.

Table 17. **Product Structure of Selected OECD Chemicals: 1988**

Percentages

	United States	Europe	Japan
Industrial Chemicals	53	56	61
Agricultural Chemicals	12	13	9
Pharmaceuticals	35	31	30
Total	100	100	100

Source: Adapted from national sources.

Pharmaceuticals, which include medicinals, prescription and non-prescription drugs, account for an estimated 33 per cent of the value of OECD production of the three chemicals sectors considered in this paper.

B. Industry Structure

The OECD chemicals industry is not as concentrated as many other industrial sectors; the top ten chemicals companies account for about 25 per cent of the value of OECD chemicals sales and 20 per cent of world sales. However, the industry has engaged in increased merger and acquisition activity in recent years in order to improve economies of scale, diversify output and move production closer to raw materials supplies and to markets. Many firms are diversifying into specialty products to shield earnings against cyclical downturns in the commodity chemicals market.

European firms dominate the chemicals market, particularly the three large German firms BASF, Hoechst and Bayer, which have long been the world's largest chemicals producers (see Table 18). Previously part of the I.G. Farben chemicals group broken up after World War II, each of these firms has its specialities: BASF in fertilizers and plastics, Hoechst in pharmaceuticals and fibers, and Bayer in pesticides and industrial chemicals. ICI of the United Kingdom and Ciba-Geigy of Switzerland rank next among Europe's chemical giants; Ciba-Geigy ranks first in the world in agrochemicals production and third in world production of pharmaceuticals.

France's two large chemicals companies, Rhone-Poulenc and Orkem (formerly CdF Chimie), are state-owned. Rhone-Poulenc is now diversifying its product profile through the acquisition of niche businesses such as Union Carbide's agrochemicals group, Stauffer's inorganic chemicals group and Monsanto's vanillin activities. Montedison, Italy's largest private chemicals firm, recently merged with the state-owned Enichem to form EniMont, a new company producing bulk industrial chemicals as well as specialty chemicals. Other large

Table 18. **Principal Chemicals Manufacturers: 1988**

Bil. US$

All chemicals		Pharmaceuticals	
Firm	Sales	Firm	Sales
BASF (Germany)	25.0	Merck (US)	5.1
Hoechst (Germany)	23.3	Glaxo (UK)	3.6
Bayer (Germany)	23.0	Ciba-Geigy (Switzerland)	3.6
ICI (UK)	20.8	Hoechst (Germany)	3.4
Du Pont (US)	14.7	American Home Products (US)	2.9
Dow Chemical (US)	12.1	Pfizer (US)	2.9
Ciba-Geigy (Switzerland)	12.1	Takeda (Japan)	2.7
Rhone-Poulenc (France)	10.9	Sandoz (Switzerland)	2.7
Montedison (Italy)	10.8	Bayer (Germany)	2.6
Exxon (US)	10.0	Eli Lilly (US)	2.5

Source: Chemical & Engineering News and OECD.

diversified European chemicals firms include Norway's Norsk Hydro which is Europe's largest fertilizer producer; the Netherland's Akzo which has a base in inorganic chemicals and is the world's largest salt producer; Belgium's Solvay, another large inorganic chemicals producer and the world's largest producer of soda ash; Sweden's Nobel Industries; and Spain's Union Explosivos Rio Tinto.

The five largest US chemicals producers are Du Pont, Dow Chemical, Exxon, Union Carbide and Monsanto. The largest purely chemicals firm is Union Carbide, where chemicals account for over 90 per cent of output, followed by Dow Chemical (73 per cent) and Monsanto (67 per cent). Although Du Pont is the United State's largest chemicals producer, chemicals account for only 45 per cent of the firm's ouput. Other large US chemicals producers are energy companies such as Exxon, Occidental Petroleum, Amoco, Mobil, Shell Oil and General Electric, where chemicals account for 15 per cent or less of output value. In Canada, Nova Corp. of Alberta is the largest chemicals firm followed by Dow, Shell, Esso and Dupont, subsidiaries of foreign corporations.

The Japanese chemicals sector is not so highly developed or diversified as the European and US industries. Japan's chemicals companies are one-fifth to one-tenth the size of western firms. The average sales of Japan's five largest chemicals companies – Asahi, Mitsubishi Kasei, Sumitomo, Toray and Sekisui – were $5 billion in 1988 compared to $20 billion for the five largest European firms and $10 billion for the five largest US firms. Japanese firms are now reorienting towards export markets and entering into mergers, acquisitions and partnerships with small foreign companies.

The pharmaceuticals sector tends to be more highly concentrated than the overall chemicals industry in most OECD countries. World concentration levels are increasing in individual product markets with growing merger and acquisition activity among the large drug companies. The pharmaceuticals sector is comprised of a relatively small group of large multinational companies heavily involved in research and development and a few thousand smaller companies producing mostly generic and over-the-counter products. In the major European countries, the large multinationals control over 60 per cent of the domestic pharmaceuticals market. Glaxo and ICI of the United Kingdom, Hoechst and Bayer of Germany and Ciba-Geigy, Sandoz and Hoffmann-La Roche of Switzerland account for most drug sales in their home markets and also have substantial exports.

The top US pharmaceutical firms are Merck, the world's largest producer, American Home Products, Pfizer, Eli Lilly, Abbott Laboratories and SmithKline Beckman, which recently merged with the UK's Beecham to form SmithKline Beecham. In another megamerger, Bristol-Myers announced a merger with Squibb in 1989 which would make this new US company the world's second largest pharmaceutical firm. Japanese pharmaceutical firms are smaller than US and European firms, although Takeda has recently joined the world's top ten producers. The average sales of Japan's top five pharmaceutical firms – which include Sankyo, Shonogi, Yamanouchi and Tanabe – are about $1 billion per year compared to $3 billion for the top five European and US pharmaceutical firms. The top ten firms in Japan account for about 40 per cent of pharmaceutical sales.

C. Demand Trends

The world market for industrial chemicals, agricultural chemicals and pharmaceuticals was estimated at almost $500 billion in 1988. The OECD countries account for about 75 per

Table 19. **Geographic Structure of World Chemicals Market: 1988[1]**

	Industrial chemicals		Agricultural chemicals		Pharmaceuticals	
	(bil. US$)	%	(bil. US$)	%	(bil. US$)	%
United States	60	23	10	20	41	23
Europe	75	29	13	26	48	27
Japan	55	21	8	16	36	20
Other OECD	8	3	2	4	4	3
Total OECD	198	76	33	66	129	73
Non-OECD	62	24	17	34	48	27
Total	260	100	50	100	177	100

1. Estimated consumption in US$ and share of total.
Source: OECD estimates.

cent of world consumption of these chemicals (see Table 19). The European countries as a whole are the largest single market for chemical products, followed by the United States and Japan; Japan is experiencing the most rapid growth in chemicals demand in the 1980s. Non-OECD countries account for about a quarter of all chemicals consumption and a third of world demand for agricultural chemicals.

Demand trends are mixed for the chemicals industry. Demand for industrial chemicals, which are used by most other manufacturing sectors, depends on overall economic growth and is subject to cyclical downturns. Demand and production of industrial chemicals were depressed during the economic recession of the early 1980s, but industrial chemicals demand has been strong in recent years with most OECD sectors operating at very high capacity levels. In contrast, demand for agricultural chemicals has declined in the mid-1980s due to the worldwide slump in farm prices and increasing concern about environmental effects; steady growth has only been experienced in phosphate fertilizers and biological pesticides. Pharmaceuticals demand is relatively inelastic and depends on such general factors as size and composition of population, incidence of diseases and level of real income. In the 1980s, demand for pharmaceuticals has remained strong and steady worldwide.

D. Production Trends

The OECD countries account for over 75 per cent of total world production of industrial chemicals, agricultural chemicals and pharmaceuticals. World production of these chemicals is approximately 33 per cent in Europe, 27 per cent in North America, 15 per cent in Japan, 13 per cent in the communist countries (Soviet Union and Central and Eastern Europe) and 12 per cent in the developing countries. About a quarter of production in the developing countries is by OECD multinationals. In the OECD countries, the chemicals industry is among the largest manufacturing sectors contributing 10 per cent of the value of manufacturing production.

There has been steady growth in chemicals production since the difficulties of the early 1980s with this trend expected to continue in the medium term. Between 1979 and 1982, the chemicals industry experienced a deep recession due to reduced demand as well as to the oil crisis and the need to adjust to new environmental controls. In most OECD countries, the industry restructured and rationalised during the 1980s through closures, joint ventures and acquisitions, expansion into overseas markets and diversification into specialty chemicals. Current high capacity rates reflect the partial shutdown in capacity between 1982 and 1986. Since 1987, overall chemicals production in real terms has increased at a rate of 3 to 4 per cent annually in the OECD area.

The European countries as a whole are the largest producers of chemicals, led by Germany and France (see Table 20). The United Kingdom, Italy, the Netherlands and Switzerland are also important diversified producers. National shares in the output of various type of chemicals have undergone little change in Europe since the 1960s. The United States is the single largest chemicals producer accounting a third of OECD production of industrial and agricultural chemicals and pharmaceuticals and having its highest output share in pharmaceuticals. Although Japan has reduced capacity in many industrial chemicals since 1982, it remains a large producer accounting for 27 per cent of OECD production. Japan accounts for lesser shares of OECD output of agricultural chemicals (18 per cent) and pharmaceuticals (23 per cent). Canada and Australia also have sizeable chemicals industries, accounting for about 3 per cent and 1 per cent of OECD production respectively.

Table 20. **OECD Chemicals Production: 1988**

Mil. US$

	Industrial chemicals	Agricultural chemicals	Pharmaceuticals
United States	62 500	14 000	41 300
Japan	56 000	8 000	27 800
Europe	82 000	19 500	46 000
Germany	25 200	3 400	10 500
France	13 200	5 200	11 300
UK	10 000	2 050	6 900
Italy	10 500	3 500	7 000
Netherlands	8 300	2 000	1 400
Switzerland	4 500	600	5 600
Belgium	4 400	600	1 300
Finland	1 200	500	320
Norway	950	500	270
Spain	900	300	200
Portugal	750	450	190
Canada	7 300	1 400	2 500
Australia	1 150	1 000	950
Total OECD	208 950	43 900	118 550

Source: OECD estimates.

E.   Trade and Foreign Investment Trends

World trade in all chemicals reached nearly $200 billion in 1988. OECD exports of industrial chemicals, agricultural chemicals and pharmaceuticals were valued at about $115 billion in 1987 (see Table 21). Industrial chemicals are the most traded product with about 40 per cent of OECD production exported compared to export shares of 28 per cent in agricultural chemicals and 18 per cent in pharmaceuticals. A large share of the world's industrial chemical exports are accounted for by the Middle Eastern countries, particularly Saudi Arabia, Qatar and Libya. The Soviet Union, China and Morocco are among the countries which export agricultural chemicals, primarily fertilizer.

The European Community (EC) is the world's largest chemicals exporting bloc, with total exports of industrial chemicals, agricultural chemicals and pharmaceuticals valued at $85 billion in 1987, about 40 per cent of which was exported to countries outside the EC. Europe's trade surplus with the rest of the world in these chemicals is about $20 billion per year compared with a surplus of about $9 billion for the United States and a small deficit for Japan. European chemical firms export a large share of domestic production, about 75 per cent in Switzerland and 60 per cent in the United Kingdom and Germany. Italy is the only major European country with an overall deficit in chemicals trade, while France is experiencing an increasing deficit in agricultural chemicals trade due to large imports of fertilizer. European trade in pharmaceuticals has been limited through national price-setting and other regulations, but intra-EC and international competition in pharmaceuticals is expected to increase after 1992.

Table 21.   **OECD Chemicals Trade: 1987**

Mil. US$

	Industrial chemicals		Agricultural chemicals		Pharmaceuticals	
	Exports	Balance[1]	Exports	Balance	Exports	Balance
United States	11 457	4 956	4 162	3 188	3 216	421
Japan	6 405	−268	334	−133	562	−1 370
Europe	59 700		7 400		17 500	
Extra-EC	22 484		2 324		7 500	
Germany	17 505	7 420	1 754	760	3 662	1 550
France	8 931	1 230	854	−847	2 310	1 023
UK	8 352	2 109	960	387	2 467	1 240
Italy	3 495	−2 828	414	−222	1 161	−327
Netherlands	7 620	2 920	1 126	701	1 013	67
Switzerland	4 468	1 804	538	396	2 959	2 140
Canada	2 560	77	991	680	147	−293
Australia	230	48	23	−104	76	−270
Total OECD	80 452		12 910		21 500	

1. Trade Balance = exports minus imports.
Source: OECD.

The United States increased its share of the global chemicals market in 1988 after a three-year decline in market share. US firms export about 15 per cent of chemicals output varying from 30 per cent of agricultural chemicals production to 8 per cent of pharmaceuticals production. The positive US trade balance in chemicals has been shrinking since 1980 but showed some improvement in 1987-1988. The US trade balance in industrial chemicals has declined to $5 billion primarily due to capacity constraints in US industry and increasing imports of ethylene and other organic chemicals. The US trade surplus in agricultural chemicals is due largely to its position as the world's largest producer of phosphate fertilizers; the US share of the world pesticide market has declined from 30 per cent in 1985 to 22 per cent in 1988. The declining US trade surplus in pharmaceuticals led to an almost neutral trade balance in 1988.

Japan's chemicals industry is oriented to the domestic market and less than 10 per cent of production is exported. Most exports are industrial chemicals. Japan accounts for 6 per cent of OECD exports of industrial and agricultural chemicals and pharmaceuticals. Japan has a deficit in total chemicals trade, particularly in pharmaceuticals where exports account for only 2 per cent of production. It is only in the 1980s that Japanese firms have started entering foreign markets. In pharmaceuticals, the United States is Japan's largest trading partner accounting for about 26 per cent of both exports and imports, followed by Germany with 10 per cent of exports and 22 per cent of imports.

Canada's overall trade in chemicals changed from negative in the period 1985 to 1987 to positive in 1988; total chemicals exports increased 26 per cent from 1987. Canada is a net exporter of industrial and agricultural chemicals but a net importer of pharmaceuticals. Most chemicals trade is with the United States, which accounts for about 63 per cent of exports and 75 per cent of imports. Australia has an overall chemicals trade deficit, which is most pronounced in pharmaceuticals, but a positive trade balance in industrial chemicals. Australian production of industrial chemicals is largely foreign-owned with exports accounting for about a fifth of turnover.

Most OECD trade in chemicals (about 70 per cent) is with other OECD countries (see Table 22). Approximately 28 per cent of OECD industrial chemicals exports, 37 per cent of agricultural chemicals exports and 27 per cent of pharmaceuticals exports are to non-OECD countries. The European countries account for about 60 per cent of OECD exports to non-OECD countries. And exports to non-OECD countries account for over 60 per cent of Europe's chemicals exports to non-European countries. Similarly, exports to non-OECD countries account for over 50 per cent of Japan's total exports of these chemicals. The United States exports relatively less -about 38 per cent of total exports - to non-OECD countries. US non-OECD chemicals exports go to Latin America (45 per cent), Asia (39 per cent) and Africa (5 per cent).

Six newly-industrialising economies (NIEs) - South Korea, Taiwan, Singapore, Hong Kong, Brazil and Mexico -account for 8 per cent of OECD chemicals exports and 28 per cent of OECD exports of chemicals to non-OECD countries. Most chemicals exports to the NIEs are industrial chemicals. Almost a third of all Japan's chemicals exports are to the NIEs. Exports of finished pharmaceuticals products to the NIEs are relatively low; many Asian and Latin American countries import active ingredients and carry out the later stages of manufacture themselves. The largest export markets for OECD pharmaceutical products are in Africa and the Middle East where local industries are weak or non-existent.

Foreign investment in the chemicals industry, which has traditionally manufactured in a few key places and exported to the rest of the world, is increasing in the 1980s. Most foreign investment by OECD firms has been in other OECD countries, but large OECD chemicals

	Industrial chemicals		Agricultural chemicals		Pharmaceuticals	
	Non-OECD	NIEs[2]	Non-OECD	NIEs	Non-OECD	NIEs
United States	21	35	38	57	13	17
Europe	56	35	48	26	82	62
Japan	16	28	5	4	4	17
Other	7	2	9	13	1	4
Total (%)	100	100	100	100	100	100
Total (mil US$)	22 350	8 000	4 820	740	5 760	580

1. Share of total OECD chemicals exports to non-OECD countries (including NIEs) and to NIEs.
2. NIEs – Newly-industrialising economies of South Korea, Taiwan, Singapore, Hong Kong, Brazil and Mexico.
Source: OECD.

firms are now stepping up non-OECD investment particularly in the Asian countries due to their projected market growth. European chemicals firms invested about $40 billion abroad in 1988, about 75 per cent of this in the United States. Foreign investment by US chemicals companies was about $30 billion in 1988; cumulative US chemicals investment overseas is $310 billion while cumulative foreign investment in the US chemicals industry has increased to over $260 billion. Foreign-owned firms, primarily European, now account for over 15 per cent of US chemical sales through local production.

Foreign investment by the Japanese chemicals industry has been slowly growing since the early 1980s, but still amounts to only 3 per cent of total Japanese foreign investment or less than $2 billion. Japanese chemicals firms are restructuring to move production of commodity items offshore, particularly to the Asian NIEs, and maintain domestic production of specialty chemicals. Japanese chemicals firms are also seeking investment opportunities and joint ventures in Europe in anticipation of the 1992 single market. Many US and European firms, including Bayer, Du Pont, Hoechst, ICI and Monsanto, are constructing factories and research facilities in Japan.

Foreign investment in pharmaceuticals is the most extensive of any segment of the chemicals industry due to the differentiation of markets and varying national regulations and standards for pharmaceutical products. It is estimated that foreign direct investment accounts for twice the value of pharmaceuticals products which enter into international trade. Most large pharmaceutical firms maintain production or assembly facilities wherever there are markets; multinational operations have helped pharmaceutical firms overcome obstacles to exports and recover high R&D costs.

Direct foreign investment in Europe's pharmaceuticals sector is relatively high. Pharmaceuticals produced locally by foreign firms account for about 90 per cent of the value of output in Belgium, 60 per cent in Spain, 50 per cent in France, Italy and Austria, and 35 per cent in the United Kingdom. Germany, the Netherlands and the Scandanavian countries are hosts to fewer foreign pharmaceuticals firms, which account for 20 per cent or less of output. Much foreign investment in Europe is by US and Swiss firms; almost 20 per cent or $9 billion of the worldwide sales of US pharmaceutical firms were by subsidiaries producing overseas, and over 50 per cent of the sales of Swiss pharmaceutical firms were by overseas subsidiaries. Swiss firms dominate their small local market, while foreign firms now account for about 18 per cent of US pharmaceutical production.

Foreign firms account for about 15 per cent of Japan's pharmaceuticals production; this share is growing rapidly with increasing investments by OECD companies in Japan. In 1988, Japanese pharmaceuticals companies had 15 production facilities in the United States, 14 in Taiwan and 11 in Europe while there were 97 foreign-owned pharmaceuticals firms operating in Japan.

The pharmaceuticals industry in Canada and Australia is largely foreign-owned with foreign firms accounting for 65 per cent or more of the value of output. Research and development in pharmaceuticals is also being internationalised; of the 30 largest drug companies, 23 have foreign R&D facilities in the United States, 16 in the United Kingdom, 11 in France, 7 in Germany and 7 in Italy.

III. MAJOR COMPETITIVE FACTORS

A. Research and Development

Competition in specialty chemicals - agricultural chemicals and pharmaceuticals - is based largely on product innovation and product differentiation rather than on price. In contrast, competition in many industrial chemicals, which are commodity or bulk items, is based more on price. Most agrochemical and pharmaceutical firms devote a small share of revenues to manufacturing costs and a large share to research and development and marketing. Because they are research-intensive and marketing-intensive, these specialty chemicals sectors give great importance to patents and trademarks.

Total R&D expenditures in the OECD chemicals sector were $23 billion in 1985 rising to about $27 billion in 1988 (see Table 23). Research and development expenditures on chemicals has averaged 10 per cent of all OECD R&D expenditures and 18 per cent of business R&D expenditures in recent years. The share of total R&D spending devoted to chemicals (over 20 per cent) is highest in Belgium, the Netherlands and Germany. Government funding of chemicals R&D varies by country but is generally higher in chemicals sectors other than pharmaceuticals, where R&D is the domain of private firms.

The European countries account for 45 per cent of OECD research expenditures in chemicals other than pharmaceuticals and 40 per cent of OECD research expenditures in pharmaceuticals. Total European chemicals research expenditures were estimated at $10 billion in 1985 rising to $12 billion in 1988. Most European research is conducted in Germany, France, the United Kingdom and Switzerland. Countries of medium technological capacity in chemicals and pharmaceuticals include Italy, the Netherlands, Belgium and Sweden. Research patterns have varied in Europe with Germany and France emphasizing chemicals research with pharmaceuticals research as a by-product, and the United Kingdom and Switzerland placing more emphasis on pharmaceuticals research linked to work in food products and biotechnology.

US R&D expenditures in chemicals and pharmaceuticals rose from about $8 billion in 1985 to over $10 billion in 1988; approximately half of this was spent in the pharmaceuticals sector. The US Government funds 5 per cent of research in basic chemicals, mostly through the Department of Defense. Japan's chemicals research expenditures were just over $4 billion in 1985 rising to about $5 billion in 1988. US and European firms have long outspent their Japanese counterparts in chemicals R&D, which has only recently intensified in Japan. In the past, the use of licensed technology promoted an emphasis on developmental rather than basic research and weak patent protection led to a focus on process rather than product research among Japanese firms.

Table 23. **Business R&D Expenditures by Country: 1985**

	Chemicals[1]	Govt.[2]	Pharmaceuticals	Govt.[2]
	(mil US$)	%	(mil US$)	%
Australia	48	0	–	–
Austria	40	6	26	5
Belgium	286	2	97	9
Canada	140	4	48	2
Denmark	19	1	56	2
Finland[3]	52	2	25	–
France	1 012	6	822	1
Germany	3 027	3	1 126	–
Ireland	9	11	10	5
Italy	292	5	454	8
Japan	2 678	1	1 525	1
Portugal	13	5	2	6
Norway	31	1	15	2
Spain	79	2	67	3
Sweden	128	12	207	1
Switzerland	600	–	732	–
United Kingdom	694	2	710	0
United States	4 648	5	3 381	0
Total OECD	13 796		9 303	

1. All chemicals other than pharmaceuticals.
2. Share of R&D expenditures funded by government.
3. Government-funded share is for both chemicals and pharmaceuticals.
Source: OECD.

Examination of R&D expenditures by firm may give a more accurate profile of chemicals research owing to the multinational nature of this industry and the large share of research conducted abroad (see Table 24). Specialty chemicals - primarily pharmaceuticals and agricultural chemicals - are among the most R&D intensive industries, along with electronics and scientific instruments; developers of specialty chemicals spend an average 10 to 12 per cent of turnover on R&D. Diversified chemicals firms, which also produce industrial chemicals and other products which are not highly R&D-intensive, spend an average 4 to 6 per cent of turnover on R&D. R&D expenditures of the five largest Japanese chemicals companies averaged $185 million in 1988, about one fourth of the average for the five largest US firms and one-fifth that of the five largest European firms.

Different trends influence research in the various chemicals sectors. Much research in the pharmaceuticals sector is directed to combining biotechnology with more traditional techniques to develop new drugs for the 1990s. Among agricultural chemicals, herbicides command the highest share of research funding (about 50 per cent of all research expenditures on pesticides) and have demonstrated the greatest technological progress. A large portion of research in industrial chemicals is being focused on environmental-related R&D; approximately 20 to 30 per cent of the investment budgets of the major chemicals firms is directed to environmental research and protection measures.

Table 24. **R&D Expenditures by Firm: 1988**

All chemicals			Pharmaceuticals		
Firm	mil US$	% of Sales	Firm	mil US$	% of Sales
BASF	1 017	4.1	Merck	650	12.7
Hoechst	1 373	5.9	Glaxo	540	15.0
Bayer	1 398	6.1	Ciba-Geigy	382	10.6
ICI	1 005	4.8	Hoechst	527	15.5
Du Pont	1 319	9.0	Sandoz	380	14.1
Ciba-Geigy	1 231	10.2	Eli-Lilly	320	12.8
Dow Chemical	772	6.4	Bayer	585	15.0
Rhone-Poulenc	641	5.9	Pfizer	473	16.3
Montedison	390	2.7	Abbott	189	8.2
Akzo	409	4.9	American Home Prod	145	5.0

Source: *Chemical and Engineering News* and OECD.

B. Patents

Patents are the commercial lifeblood of R&D-based industries such as chemicals. Patents are a legal right of ownership in inventions; other types of intellectual property rights include trademarks and copyrights. Chemicals firms depend on patent protection, and to a lesser extent trademark protection, in both domestic and foreign markets to earn an adequate return from their research expenditures. Several factors in the 1980s are increasingly eroding returns to chemicals patents, including: 1) registration and testing delays, 2) generic products and 3) patent infringement.

Patents provide legal protection for inventions granting the patent owner the right to exclude others from making, using and/or selling the invention for a limited period of time. The primary rationale for patent protection is that a period of market exclusivity is necessary to provide inventors with an incentive to invent and to disclose their inventions to the public, thus facilitating the generation and diffusion of knowledge. In the absence of legal protection, an invention can often be quickly imitated once it has been introduced to the market. Imitators can charge lower prices than the inventor because they have not incurred the same research and development costs. Such imitation reduces returns to the inventor as well as his incentive to invest resources in R&D and the generation of new technology.

The market exclusivity granted by patents to inventors may cause short-run inefficiencies usually associated with monopolies - higher prices, restricted output and inefficient resource allocation. Some maintain that patents create unnecessary barriers to entry to industries such as pharmaceuticals and give firms substantial market power and the ability to command inordinately high prices. However, other studies show that monopolies granted patent-holders are generally short-lived given the rapid dissemination of information and development of rival products. The costs incurred to society through patent awards are balanced by the long-run benefits of continuing investment in new inventions.

One cause of erosion to patent returns is the increasing difficulty of meeting government regulatory requirements for chemicals products and the degree to which time needed for testing and registration decreases the term of patent protection. Approval procedures are becoming more onerous and expensive due to increased public interest in the health and safety problems associated with new chemicals and drugs. Several years may be required after a patent application is filed or a patent is issued for technical and market development and regulatory approval before a new chemicals product can be marketed. In many countries, the patent term keeps running while such regulatory approvals are obtained, resulting in an effectively shorter period of time during which the product can be marketed under patent protection. The European Community has estimated that registration delays in the different European countries reduce the effective life of a pharmaceuticals patent from the original 20 years to about 9 years, and US studies indicate that the profitable lifetime of a new drug has decreased to less than 8 years. The United States and Japan have recently extended the patent protection granted to pharmaceuticals to compensate for the time required to obtain government pre-market approvals.

Another cause of erosion of returns to pharmaceutical patents is the increasing sale of generic products. Generics are less expensive copies of usually brand-name drugs whose patents have expired. They now account for almost a third of the prescription drug market in the United States and Europe and their share continues to grow. Government health agencies and insurance organisations, who are the main purchasers of pharmaceuticals in many OECD countries, are encouraging physicians to prescribe more generic medicines in an effort to reduce health care costs. Many brand-name products, which could often maintain 80 per cent of their sales for several years after patent expiration, now face increasing competition from generic drugs. R&D-intensive pharmaceutical firms maintain generics reduce the revenues they need to compensate their high research costs; however, many of the major producers (e.g., Ciba-Geigy, American Cyanamid, American Home Products) have started their own generic drug divisions. Generic drug producers, mostly small companies, are also forming their own trade associations in OECD countries.

A third source of erosion to patent returns in the 1980s is patent infringement by companies which illegally imitate and market patented chemicals products. Unauthorised use of patents worldwide has grown partly due to increasing trade and foreign investment in chemicals products and the development of technology for imitating chemicals. Because they have incurred no research and development costs, pirate firms sell products at lower prices reducing the patent owner's sales volume and return on investment. Although there are also patent problems in the OECD countries, unauthorised use of chemicals patents most frequently occurs in non-OECD countries owing to the nature of their patent protection systems (see Table 25). In many cases, patent systems in non-OECD countries have the goal of speeding the transfer and diffusion of technology and promoting access to foreign technology in the interest of economic development.

One main difference in patent systems is the type of patentable subject matter allowed. Product or compound-per-se patents cover a specific chemical structure and are the strongest form of patent protection for chemicals products. However, some maintain that product patents block the development of chemicals products by alternative processes and are too restrictive. Many countries offer process patents covering the manufacturing process by which a chemical is made; process patents are easier to avoid through small changes in the production process. Countries may also offer composition patents, which cover a formulation or mixture of chemicals containing one or more active ingredients and at least one carrier. Method-of-use patents, which cover new uses for known chemicals compounds, are another type of chemicals

Table 25. **Patent System Features for Chemicals Products: 1988**

Feature	Examples of Non-OECD Countries
Provides patents for processes but not products	Mexico, Argentina, Chile, Venezuela, India
Excludes pharmaceuticals and agrochemicals	Brazil, Thailand
Compulsory licensing	Taiwan, Singapore, Malaysia, Venezuela
Compulsory working	Mexico, Brazil, Thailand, Argentina, Chile
Short patent term	Columbia, India
Limited patent dispute settlement procedures	Korea, Taiwan, Singapore
No legal mechanisms for detecting processes used to make competitive products	Argentina, Chile

Source: OECD.

patent, but are not available in many countries. In some countries, specialty chemicals such as pharmaceuticals and agricultural chemicals may be excluded from all forms of patent protection.

Patent systems may contain compulsory licensing and/or working provisions. Compulsory licensing requires a patentee to license his patent to another producer who wishes to use it, sometimes at a low royalty rate set by the government. Such licences are usually granted on specific grounds, such as the failure of the patentee to work his invention to satisfy a demand. Compulsory working requires a patentee or his licensee to work or commercially exploit the patent in the country within a certain time period or suffer patent cancellation or compulsory licensing. Working provisions can be troublesome when timeframes are short relative to the time needed to obtain government marketing approvals. Other patent system features which may cause problems to OECD chemicals firms are inadequate patent terms, lack of effective judicial and enforcement procedures to deal with patent infringement issues and lack of legal means for detecting and ruling on infringing chemicals processes.

C. Patent Licensing

The chemicals industry engages in licensing perhaps to a greater extent than any other industrial sector. For the most part, this licensing is based on patents and involves the transfer of product or process technology or distribution rights in exchange for royalties or fees. Licensing is an important competitive strategy for chemicals firms seeking to increase returns to research and development, to exploit small or inaccessible geographic markets and to gain complementary technical information. Trading in patent rights through licensing is popular in the chemicals industry, both nationally and internationally. Much chemicals licensing takes place between associated firms linked by equity holdings and with subsidiaries.

Patent licensing, and particularly certain licensing techniques and restrictions, may act to create monopolies which inhibit competition and raise prices for consumers. Some believe that chemical firms which license their technology with restrictive clauses extend their market power beyond that warranted by the innovation itself. Restrictions on price, output, territories and field of use and features such as package licensing, tie-in sales, exclusivity requirements and refusals to license are among the techniques which may contribute to anticompetitive effects. However, recent work by the OECD indicates that patent licensing, like patents in general, is a legitimate instrument for allowing firms to capture returns from their technology and to encourage further innovative activity. The various types of restrictions associated with patent licensing may promote or reduce competition depending on the circumstances. The OECD Council recently adopted a recommendation cancelling an earlier one concerning the use of patents and licences and advised that the competitive effects of licensing agreements be reviewed on a case-by-case basis.

Trends in patents (number of patent applications or grants) and patent licensing (trade balances in licensing royalties and fees) are sometimes used as measures of industrial competitiveness. Patents themselves are an unreliable guide to either innovation or competitiveness largely because patent systems and practices differ significantly by country. For example, Japanese firms file a far greater number of patent applications for chemicals and other inventions both at home and abroad than US or European firms (see Table 26). It is estimated that Japanese firms now account for 20 per cent of new chemicals patents issued in the United States and 12 per cent of those issued in Europe. However, Japanese firms tend to file applications for narrow claims; they also have a higher percentage of licensed products in their development pipeline which do not incur basic research expenses and are follow-up products rather than original chemical entities. In general, patent data are a poor indicator of competitiveness because they lack information on the significance of the invention, the R&D investment and the product's ultimate commercial success.

Patent licensing statistics may be a better indicator of competitiveness because they show the directional flows of technology. In the past, the United States and several European countries have been net exporters of chemicals technology based on patent licensing while Japan has been a net importer. For the United States, United Kingdom and Germany, royalties and fee receipts from chemicals licensing are estimated to be as much as 20 per cent of business R&D expenditures on chemicals. For many years, Japan's payments for patent licenses were over 25 per cent of R&D expenditures in chemicals resulting in a continuing deficit in its technology balance of payments for chemicals. But Japan has used licensed patents to successfully build its chemicals industry and is becoming a net exporter rather than importer of technology; in 1989, Japan should have a surplus on its chemicals patent licensing account. In general, Japanese chemicals firms are reducing their dependence on licensed technology due

Table 26. **Trends in OECD Patent Applications**

	1982		1987	
	Total	Foreign[1] %	Total	Foreign %
United States	112 234	44	133 451	49
Japan	238 880	12	343 984	10
Germany	71 262	56	79 074	59

1. Share of national patent applications filed by foreign concerns.
Source: OECD.

to both the declining availability of patent licenses and the goal of increasing profit ratios through domestically-developed products.

Patent licensing has been particularly widespread in pharmaceuticals owing to marketing difficulties; most drugs have to be made known to individual doctors which requires huge sales forces. Licensing allows firms to use their sales personnel to market foreign products or to give another firm the right to sell its product in exchange for a royalty. However, in the past few years, there has been a trend to more direct marketing in pharmaceuticals so as to increase earnings. For example, almost 50 per cent of the pharmaceuticals consumed in Japan are under foreign-owned patents, but only 20 per cent are sold by the foreign firms themselves. Western firms are now attempting to increase their own sales networks in Japan; Ciba-Geigy, SmithKline Beecham and Glaxo are among the firms who have bought out their former licensing and joint-venture partners in Japan. Similarly, Japanese pharmaceutical firms are moving to direct marketing in foreign markets; Cardizem, Pepcid and Cefobid are all important Japanese drugs known to Americans under the labels of Marion, Merck and Pfizer but which may soon be sold under Japanese labels. US and Japanese pharmaceutical firms are also building distribution channels and sales networks in Europe in anticipation of the single market.

Most patent licensing in the chemicals industry is in the OECD area as the nature or uncertainty of patent and trademark protection in non-OECD countries often acts as a disincentive to licensing. OECD chemicals firms also cite other patent licensing problems in non-OECD countries, including foreign exchange controls on royalty payments and fees, requirements for prior government approval or registration of licenses, and obligations to disclose patent information to obtain government licensing approval.

IV. INDUSTRIAL AND TRADE POLICIES

Although the OECD countries maintain a floor of certain minimum standards of protection for patents and other forms of intellectual property, the differences in OECD patent systems cause difficulties for chemicals firms that operate internationally (see Table 27). Variations in the scope, duration and other features of OECD patent systems and the shortcomings of international patent conventions in bridging these differences may contribute to the reduction in economic returns to chemicals and pharmaceutical patents.

The United States, Japan and the European Patent Convention provide product patents for chemicals and pharmaceuticals. Several OECD countries were late in offering product patents – Japan in 1975 and Italy in 1978 – and some European countries – Finland, Spain, Portugal and Yugoslavia – do not offer full product patent protection for both chemicals and pharmaceuticals; Spain and Portugal will offer product protection for chemicals and pharmaceuticals from 1992. With the exception of the United States, most OECD countries provide for compulsory licenses for non-working of chemicals patents in accordance with the provisions of the Paris Convention; however, these provisions are seldom acted upon partly because they foster a climate in which voluntary licensing is encouraged.

The US patent system is based on a first-to-invent principle while those of the European Patent Convention, Japan and most other countries are based on a first-to-file principle; the United States has indicated willingness to adopt a first-to-file system in negotiating international patent rules. The first-to-invent system may involve expensive and lengthy interference proceedings to prove prior inventorship, while the first-to-file system encourages a more rapid disclosure of inventions. Patent terms differ by area: 20 years in Europe (from the filing date of the application under the EPC), 17 years in the United States (from patent grant) and 15 years in Japan (from publication of the examined patent application). The United States grants up to a five-year patent extension to pharmaceuticals and animal drugs to allow for premarket reviews, while Japan allows a five-year extension for pharmaceuticals and agrochemicals and Europe is considering proposals for patent extensions for some products. In the United States, legislation has been under consideration for several years to allow patent term extension for agricultural chemicals subject to pre-market approval.

Although all three systems now allow multiple claims, Japan only recently made this change and the scope of Japanese patents remains more narrow than in the United States and Europe. Japanese patent applications are more specific to support the preferred Japanese standard of a single invention in a single application. US and European patent applications are often written with inclusive language and generalised examples to support broad claims. Japanese applicants have found it difficult to combine their specific disclosures to support the more comprehensive multiple-claim US and European systems, while Western applicants in

83

Table 27. **Comparison of OECD Patent Systems**

	United states	Europe [1]	Japan
Type	First-to-invent	First-to-file	First-to-file
Term	17 years (from patent grant)	20 years (from application filing)	15 years (from publication)
Extensions	Pharmaceuticals Animal Drugs	None	Pharmaceuticals Agrochemicals
Scope	Broad	Leaning to broad	Narrow
Publication prior to grant	None	18-month	18-month
Opposition	Postgrant	Postgrant	Pre- and postgrant
Filing	Inventor filing	Assignee filing	Assignee filing
Grace period	One year	None	Six months (limited)

1. European Patent Convention (European countries also have national patent systems which may differ in some respects from the EPC).
Source: OECD.

Japan have had difficulty supporting their claims with the specificity and fullness of disclosure required by the Japanese Patent Office.

Another important difference in OECD patent systems are rules regarding publication of patents. In the United States, a patent application is secret until a patent is issued. In Europe, Japan and most other countries, patent applications are published 18 months or so after filing. The earlier dissemination of information through publication is intended to encourage others to develop from it and reduces the duplication of research effort. US firms maintain that publication gives other companies access to their technology and encourages rivals to file competing patents. In the United States and Europe, opposition or re-examination procedures are limited to after the patent has been granted. The United States requires that inventors file patent applications, while in other countries an assignee or legal recipient of the patent right may file. Only the United States and Canada give an inventor a one-year grace period in which to file a patent application after an invention is publically disclosed; most other countries have either no grace period or a shorter grace period under limited circumstances.

A. United States

US patent laws most strongly favour the rights of the inventor, and the United States is pursuing both multilateral and bilateral negotiations to strengthen international intellectual property rights protection as well as working to reinforce its domestic laws. In the last decade, the United States enacted legislation establishing a single court of appeals for patent cases, a process patent bill to prevent imports of products produced by unauthorised use of patented processes, and patent term restoration for pharmaceuticals and animal drugs.

Recent legislation has contributed to raising the profile of international intellectual property rights issues in the United States. The Trade and Tariff Act of 1984 amended section 301 of the Trade Act of 1974 to allow the imposition of import restrictions against countries that inadequately protect US intellectual property. In 1988, in response to a complaint filed by the US Pharmaceutical Manufacturers Association, the United States invoked these provisions in imposing punitive tariffs on certain Brazilian exports in retaliation for Brazil's lack of patent protection for American pharmaceuticals; this case is now being considered by a GATT dispute settlement panel at the request of Brazil.

The same act also amended the Generalized System of Preferences (GSP) - a programme which allows developing countries to export designated products to the United States duty-free to further their economic development - to require that intellectual property protection be considered in determining a country's eligibility under the GSP programme. Mexico amended its patent law in 1986 after the United States eliminated $400 million in Mexican exports from the GSP programme. In 1988, the United States eliminated $165 million of Thailand's $350 million in GSP benefits due to Thailand's failure to provide adequate intellectual property protection for pharmaceuticals and computer programmes. US trade officials have also engaged in bilateral negotiations with several developing countries to encourage them to enact stronger intellectual property rights laws and to enforce them more vigorously. These talks resulted in amended laws and, to a lesser extent, more vigorous enforcement in countries such as South Korea, Taiwan and Singapore.

The Omnibus Trade and Competitiveness Act of 1988 authorized the US Trade Representative to identify priorities under Section 301 of the Trade Act for the initiation of negotiations with countries which use alleged unfair trade practices; in addition, special procedures provide for the identification of priority countries which do not adequately protect patents and other forms of intellectual property or unfairly close their markets to US firms that rely on intellectual property protection. Under these procedures, the United States announced a priority watch list of countries with whom negotiations on intellectual property rights would be intensified: Brazil, India, Korea, Mexico, China, Saudi Arabia, Taiwan and Thailand. In addition, 17 other countries, including 7 OECD countries, were placed on a watch list with which the United States will increase efforts to resolve any problems relating to intellectual property rights.

The 1988 Trade Act also amended the Tariff Act of 1930 to remove a requirement that domestic firms prove injury prior to filing complaints against foreign companies for violating intellectual property rights under Section 337. In 1988, a GATT dispute panel established in 1986 at the behest of the European Community concluded that certain procedures under Section 337 are inconsistent with the GATT in that they accord to imported products challenged as infringing US patents less favourable treatment than that accorded to US products.

B.   Japan

The Japanese patent system was revised in 1975 to offer more comprehensive patent protection for chemicals and pharmaceuticals and subsequent provisions have been enacted to provide patent extensions for pharmaceuticals and to move to a multiple claims system.

A number of factors have led to a very high rate of patent application filing in Japan: the first-to-file system, the tradition of narrow rather than broad claims, the low cost of a patent application, the great prestige attached to filing and receiving patents, and the practice of defensive patenting as a means to block competitors. Japanese firms file annually three times as many patents as European firms and four times as many patents as US firms with their national patent offices. In Japan, only about half of the patent applications filed are granted and of these, only 10 to 15 per cent are put to use. The Japanese patent system is essentially designed to stimulate industrial development and to foster cooperation and cross-licensing.

Many Western firms maintain that the Japanese patent system favours Japanese firms and leads to coerced licensing of technology. The publication of patent applications, the pre-grant opposition procedures and the large number of Japanese patent applications lead to what is termed ''patent flooding'' causing the inventor of the original product to license the technology to Japanese firms. Western firms also fault the inadequate number of Japanese patent examiners in view of the number of applications received and the delays in patent reviews and grants. The Japanese patent system is especially difficult for small and medium-sized companies to negotiate. However, it is unclear to what extent foreign firms may not have adapted their operations sufficiently to the rules and style of the Japanese patent system.

Japan supports the harmonisation of intellectual property rights and patent systems at the international level through multilateral negotiations. Japan protested US bilateral negotiations with South Korea which led to a chemical product patent system in South Korea which is seen as initially favouring US firms. Japan and the United States have held bilateral talks concerning trade-related patent problems and formed a working group on intellectual property in 1988 to discuss patent issues such as patent infringement and delays in granting patents. Japan and the European Community have held bilateral talks to discuss market access for EC pharmaceutical products, including mutual acceptance of test results and certification.

C. Europe

The European Community is attempting to establish a single patent enforceable in all EC countries by yearend 1992. At present, the 12 member nations of the European Community each have their own intellectual property rights and patent systems, which create delays and difficulties for European as well as foreign firms. Although firms can now obtain patents in all member countries through a single application to the European Patent Office (which includes Sweden, Switzerland, Austria, Liechtenstein and the EC countries except Ireland and Portugal), enforcement of such patents must by pursued on a country-by-country basis.

The European Community is also developing a common policy on trade-related intellectual property rights issues. In 1984, a common commercial policy instrument (Article 113) was enacted to allow retaliation in the case of unfair trade practices such as patent infringement; any action under this article must first go through applicable GATT procedures. In 1987, the European Community suspended general tariff preferences for South Korean products because of inadequate protection for the intellectual property of European firms.

Proposals are being considered by the European Community to accelerate registration procedures and harmonise price-setting rules for pharmaceuticals. A pan-European registration regime is proposed which would set up a centralised authority to deal with all new formulations while existing national bodies would continue to consider variations on existing products. Another proposal is to introduce a system of mutual recognition under which countries accept each other's rulings on whether new formulations should be permitted for sale. The EC also hopes to achieve some convergence in drug pricing which now varies greatly by country; a transparency directive to be implemented in January 1990 establishes that all price setting rules should follow published criteria which are clear and objective.

D.   Other OECD

Amendments to the Canadian Patent Act in 1987 changed the patent system from a first-to-invent to a first-to-file system, altered the term of a patent from 17 years from the date of the grant to 20 years from the filing date, and introduced patent maintenance fees. Prior to 1987, Canada also had a compulsory licensing system for pharmaceuticals that allowed generic drug companies to produce and sell copies of patented drugs by paying a 4 per cent royalty fee to the patent holder. Compulsory licensing was introduced in 1969 largely to maintain low prices for pharmaceuticals. Under the revised system, new pharmaceuticals receive seven years of protection against licensing and benefit from the lengthened patent term.

E.   Non-OECD Countries

Infringement or unauthorised use of OECD chemicals patents has occurred primarily in non-OECD countries owing to the nature of their patent protection systems and their increasing technical and industrial capabilities for producing chemical and pharmaceutical products. In the 1980s, surveys of OECD firms indicate that infringement of chemical patents is most frequent in the following countries: Taiwan, South Korea, Mexico, Brazil, Thailand, Argentina, Chile, Singapore, Indonesia and India. These and a few other countries have been the predominant sources of pirated chemical and pharmaceutical products both sold within those countries and exported to other markets.

There have been significant moves toward stronger patent protection in some newly-industrialising economies (NIEs) both in response to the perception that intellectual property protection is necessary to stimulate industrial development and to pressure from OECD governments. Both South Korea and Taiwan amended their patent laws in 1986 to grant product patents to chemicals and to extend patent terms. However, Taiwan still has extensive compulsory licensing, and dispute settlement procedures in both countries are weak. Mexico extended process patents to chemicals in 1986 and will also give product patent protection in the future; however, Mexican patent law contains provisions for patent lapse if a product is not worked within two years, compulsory licensing after a six-month lapse in working, and public divulgence of detailed product information upon registration application.

Malaysia implemented a new patent law in 1986 covering pharmaceutical and chemical products but maintained compulsory licensing provisions although with reasonable compensation to patent holders. In 1990, the Chilean government enacted a new pharmaceuticals patent law after a complaint filed in the United States by the Pharmaceuticals Manufacturers Association. Indonesia will enact its first patent law in late 1989; the draft legislation includes compulsory licensing and working provisions.

Most other countries have a patent law of some kind, but may fail to provide product patents for chemicals and pharmaceuticals. China is considering legislation to protect pharmaceutical patents by 1990. Singapore does not provide full patent protection to chemicals and pharmaceuticals; the Singapore Government reserves the right to use pharmaceutical patents without authorisation in hospitals and for other purposes. India gives process patents to chemicals for a limited patent term of 5 to 7 years. Argentina and Venezuela give process patents to chemicals, require patents to be worked in the country within two years or become invalid and allow compulsory licensing with limited royalties. Neither Brazil nor Thailand provide patent protection for pharmaceuticals and both have been the subject of retaliatory action by the US Government for failure to protect US intellectual property rights.

V. MAJOR POLICY ISSUES

A. Economic Costs of Patent Infringement

Patent infringement can cause substantial economic losses to the holders of patents due to lost sales in domestic markets, lost sales in foreign markets, reduced licensing fees and royalties, enforcement costs and general downward pressure on product prices. The International Chamber of Commerce estimates the annual costs of infringement of all forms of intellectual property rights to the holders of these rights at about $70 billion in recent years or 3 per cent of the value of world merchandise trade. There are substantial difficulties in estimating the economic costs of intellectual property rights infringement due to problems in identifying counterfeit or pirated products, estimating lost sales of legitimate goods at higher prices, extrapolating from one country or product to worldwide effects and quantifying intangible costs. However, the increasing seriousness of the problem has prompted several surveys of firms and industries and attempts to quantify IPR-related economic losses in recent years.

Surveys shows that the chemicals industry may account for about 10 per cent of total losses due to intellectual property rights infringement or $7 billion to $8 billion per year; in the case of chemicals, this is primarily due to unauthorised use of patents (see Table 28). These estimates are based on worldwide sales of patented chemicals products and are generally compatible with other estimates of IPR-related economic losses made in the member Countries, particularly the United States. The only industries believed to experience larger IPR-related economic costs are computers and software and scientific instruments and photographic equipment. Other industries with significant losses due to intellectual property rights infringement are entertainment (e.g., records, cassettes, films, videos), electronics, motor vehicles and parts, printing and publishing and textiles and apparel.

Pharmaceutical firms incur the highest costs due to patent infringement or an estimated 5 per cent of the value of worldwide revenues. Pharmaceutical products are highly dependent on patent protection to earn sufficient returns and are also particularly susceptible to overseas pirating because of the high research-based selling prices which they command. Similarly, several agricultural chemical products, particularly herbicides, attract potential infringers because of the premium prices charged to offset high R&D expenses. Economic costs to producers of agricultural chemicals due to patent infringement are estimated at about 3 per cent of the value of worldwide sales. Producers of industrial organic and inorganic chemicals do not generally obtain patents or depend on intellectual property protection except for a limited number of products; economic costs to these firms due to both patent and trademark infringement are estimated at 0.5 per cent of the value of worldwide sales.

The cost profile of the chemicals industry due to patent infringement differs somewhat from that of other industrial sectors; most economic costs to chemicals firms are incurred in

Table 28. **Economic Costs of Chemicals Patent Infringement: 1988**

Mil US$

	Industrial Chemicals	Agricultural Chemicals	Pharmaceuticals
European firms	400	600	2 600
US firms	300	500	2 300
Japanese firms	200	100	800
OECD Total	900	1 200	5 700

Source: OECD estimates.

foreign rather than domestic markets. Domestic sales lost to imports of pirated chemicals products are estimated to account for less than 5 per cent of the losses of OECD chemicals firms due to patent infringement as compared to over 50 per cent of losses in the entertainment or software industries. Lost foreign sales in both the infringing country and third markets are estimated to account for 70 per cent or more of the losses to OECD chemicals firms due to patent infringement. Entire markets for chemical products can be lost when a country determines that a local pirate industry is sufficient to supply domestic needs and shuts out imports through ultrahigh duties or denial of import licenses.

About 15 per cent or more of the economic costs to chemicals firms derives from lost revenues from royalties and fees due to foregone patent licensing opportunities or lowered royalties. Because patent protection is especially important to chemicals firms in maintaining a high level of licensing royalties and fees, patent infringement can severely reduce this revenue source. Another 10 per cent of total economic costs results from expenditures on identifying, detecting and combating patent infringement in domestic and foreign markets. In addition to these direct costs to chemicals firms, the use of ineffective or harmful pirated chemicals products poses serious health and safety risks to consumers and can lead to further economic losses. For example, a counterfeit of a Chevron fungicide resulted in the destruction of the major portion of the 1979-80 coffee crop in Kenya.

B. R&D Effects of Patent Infringement

Economic losses to technology-based firms owing to infringement of patents and other forms of intellectual property rights can reduce returns to research and development and lead to a decline in investments in research and innovative activities. Many believe technological progress is associated with a stream of innovations in key sectors that stimulate economic growth largely through intersectoral linkages. Along with the electronics industry, the chemicals industry has the highest rate of application of its innovations in other sectors; chemicals innovations are used primarily in the health, food processing, textiles and agricultural sectors. Studies show that the chemicals industry is a core technology sector along with electronics, machinery, mechanical engineering and scientific instruments.

Patent protection may have a strong effect on the willingness of chemicals firms to undertake research and development. Firms producing specialty chemicals must invest in long-term, high risk R&D as well as health and safety testing and registration and market development before any new product can be sold. R&D costs for chemicals have risen at a rate more than twice that of inflation in the past ten years due largely to the increase in demand for safety and more stringent testing requirements. It is estimated that a new pesticide now takes ten years and about $50 to $70 million to develop and register. Only one compound in 15 000 compounds that are synthesized and tested results in a new commercial agrochemical product. A new drug may take ten years and $150 to $200 million to discover, test and receive marketing approval. For every 10 000 chemicals synthesized, only 1 000 are promising enough to test on animals, of these only 10 are tested on humans, and of these perhaps one will yield a pharmaceutical product that can be marketed profitably.

Many chemicals firms rely on a small number of very successful products to generate returns and provide the revenues for research and development. Two or three products alone account for 70 to 80 per cent of total sales in some major pharmaceutical and agricultural chemical firms. Sales of pirated chemicals products in a foreign country can reduce the profit margins on a leading pesticide or drug by as much as 20 to 40 per cent. For these firms, the limited period of exclusive market position associated with patents is essential to maintaining revenues and R&D activities.

In one set of studies, the social rate of return or payoff to society of R&D investment in chemicals product innovations was found to be 71 per cent compared to a private rate of return to firms of about 9 percent, the largest differential in any industry. The patent system has its greatest effect in preventing imitation in the pharmaceuticals sector; it is estimated that patents increase imitation costs by about 30 per cent for drugs compared to 10 per cent for all chemicals and 7 per cent in electronics and machinery.

Table 29. **Sectoral Effects of Patent Protection on Innovation**[1]

Percentages

	Introduced	Developed
Pharmaceuticals	65	60
Chemicals	30	38
Petroleum	18	25
Machinery	15	17
Fabricated Metal Products	12	12
Primary Metals	8	1
Electrical Equipment	4	11
Instruments	1	1
Office Equipment	0	0
Motor Vehicles	0	0
Rubber	0	0
Textiles	0	0

1. Share of inventions that would not have been developed or commercially introduced without patent protection, based on a random sample of 100 US firms for the period 1981 to 1983.

Source: Mansfield E. (1986), "Patents and Innovation: An Empirical Study", *Management Science*, February.

A study of 100 firms in 12 industries in the United States found that patent protection was judged to be essential for the development or introduction of 30 per cent or more of inventions in only two industries - pharmaceuticals and chemicals (see Table 29). Patent protection was found to be of more limited importance in other industrial sectors. Among the pharmaceuticals firms surveyed, 65 per cent of new drugs would not have been commercially introduced and 60 per cent would not have been developed in the period 1981 to 1983 in the absence of patent production. Among the chemicals firms surveyed, 30 per cent of new chemical products would not have been commercially introduced and 38 per cent would not have been developed in the absence of patent protection.

C.   Intellectual Property Rights and Industrial Policy

Intellectual property rights are by their very nature instruments of industrial policy. Patents and other types of intellectual property rights have long been used to stimulate technological progress and industrial development. Patent and intellectual property rights systems and the nature of protection provided generally reflect the industrial policy goals of governments, particularly in regard to the generation and diffusion of new technology. Intellectual property rights can also be used to influence trade and foreign investment flows.

The role of intellectual property rights protection in industrial policies tends to vary with a nation's level of development. Industrialised nations generally have more comprehensive intellectual property rights systems to encourage and support the innovative capabilities of industry. OECD countries are largely technology suppliers and intellectual property rights laws and enforcement reflect their advanced economic state. These systems grant rights that are broad in scope, long in duration, cover many technologies and have little-used provisions for abrogating rights before the term expires. Because many developing countries lack a technological infrastructure or industrial innovation capability, they often wish to promote their industry's access to and use of technology at the lowest possible cost. As technology users and also due to the reduced priority given to intellectual property regimes, their systems tend to be less comprehensive; they grant rights which are limited in scope, short in duration, exclude key technologies and have wider, more frequently-used provisions for abrogating rights when it is deemed in the national interest.

However, the nature of intellectual property rights systems in many developing countries may hinder their industrial development through discouraging indigenous innovation, reinforcing reliance on the research capabilities of other countries and deterring foreign investment and the transfer of foreign technology and know-how. Domestic innovators and creators are penalised by poor intellectual property protection in these countries. Major research-based firms will not want to enter risky markets. Many believe the developing countries can acquire technology through licensing and joint ventures more effectively than through appropriation of property rights and patent infringement.

In general, awareness of the protection needed through a country's patent system increases with the importance of domestic relative to foreign applications for patents. It becomes in the economic interest of countries to provide stronger protection for intellectual property when the technological capability of local industry reaches a level where such protection is warranted for its own innovative products and processes. Several of the NIEs now realise that their continued economic growth may depend on the adoption of a patent system which encourages transfer of foreign technology as well as stimulates innovation by domestic firms.

At the international level, there is a move toward increased harmonization of intellectual property rights systems, including patent laws. The major international convention on patents is the Paris Convention for the Protection of Industrial Property, which covers patents, trademarks and industrial designs. Adopted in 1883, the Convention established an International (Paris) Union which currently has 92 member countries. Although patent rules are the province of individual states, member countries comply with certain standards, such as national treatment, right of priority (right of priority of 12 months to claim patent rights in member countries after filing an application in one country) and common rules with respect to imports and compulsory licensing. Within certain limitations, member countries may require compulsory licenses to prevent the abuse of patent rights that might result from the failure to work the patent in the country. The Paris Convention also permits certain exceptions to patent coverage for foods, pharmaceuticals and chemicals. The Patent Cooperation Treaty of 1970 permits applicants to file foreign patent applications directly with the patent office of their countries; by filing one application, the applicant obtains the effect of national regular filings in all Contracting States to the Treaty.

The World Intellectual Property Organisation (WIPO), which administers the Paris Convention, is currently developing a draft of a new treaty to increase the worldwide uniformity of patent laws. Issues being discussed include harmonisation of patent terms to 20 years from date of filing, formal requirements for patents, criteria for patentability and the rights conferred by a patent application. Many developing countries, including India and Brazil, believe that WIPO is the most appropriate forum for handling intellectual property rights issues.

Talks are also being conducted in the Uruguay Round of the General Agreement on Tariffs and Trade (GATT) on trade-related aspects of intellectual property rights. Most OECD countries support a GATT agreement on intellectual property rights standards owing to alleged trade distortions arising from inadequate protection in many countries. IPR-related elements which affect international trade are termed trade-related intellectual property rights or TRIPs. OECD countries see GATT as the best forum in which to handle TRIPS because, among other reasons, of its procedures based on negotiation and conciliation, its dispute settlement mechanism and the higher visibility of trade issues. It has been agreed within GATT that negotiations on TRIPS should aim at seeking a comprehensive agreement that includes adequate substantive intellectual property standards, an effective means for enforcement of such standards, and effective and expeditious dispute settlement procedures. However, it has not been agreed which international body should oversee the results of the GATT negotiations on intellectual property rights.

A three-tiered system of intellectual property rights protection based on the level of industrial development of nations is one proposal. Under this proposal, developing countries could be allowed to offer less comprehensive intellectual property protection, especially to foreign firms, in the interest of promoting their own industrial and technological development. Countries at an intermediate stage of industrial development such as the NIEs would be expected to made an expeditious transition to strong protection as their industrial development proceeds, while the industrialised countries would maintain the highest standards for intellectual property rights protection. As countries begin to participate in international high-technology trade in a meaningful way, they would move to stronger intellectual property rights systems.

In general, the OECD countries will only be able to persuade other countries to strengthen their IPR systems if those countries believe it is in their general interest. Some propose that the OECD countries use positive incentives, such as trade preferences or other economic benefits, rather than threats of trade retaliation to encourage countries to strengthen their intellectual property rights systems. The OECD countries have to maintain some type of pressure for stronger intellectual property rights protection at the international level or some countries may continue to take advantage of the protection offered their own inventions in the OECD countries without offering comparable protection in their own markets. OECD countries need to work within a multilateral framework towards a strengthened intellectual property rights system which is in the economic interest of all nations.

REFERENCES

Comanor, W.S. (1986), "The Political Economy of the Pharmaceutical Industry", *Journal of Economic Literature,* Vol. 24, September.

Kaztenbach, N. de B. (1987), "The International Protection of Technology: A Challenge for International Law Making", *Technology in Society,* Volume 9, Number 2.

Mansfield, E. (1988), "Intellectual Property, Technology, and Economic Growth", *Economic Impact,* 3.

Mogee, M. (1989), "International Trade in Chemicals: Intellectual Property Problems and Issues", report prepared in the context of the OECD Industry Division project on Internationalisation of Industrial Activities, May.

OECD (1983), *Economic Aspects of International Chemicals Control,* Paris.

OECD (1985), *The Pharmaceutical Industry: Trade Related Issues,* Paris.

OECD (1988), "A Survey of International Technology Licensing", *STI Review,* No. 4, December.

OECD (1989), *Competition Policy and Intellectual Property Rights,* Paris.

Stalson, H. (1987), *Intellectual Property Rights and U.S. Competitiveness in Trade,* National Planning Association Report.

US International Trade Commission (1988), "Economic Effects of Intellectual Property Right Infringement", *Journal of World Trade,* February.

THE INTERNATIONAL CONSTRUCTION INDUSTRY

I. SUMMARY

The international construction industry, consisting of foreign contracts for non-residential design engineering and construction, includes a mixture of manufacturing and non-manufacturing activities. However, the international construction industry confronts trade problems similar to those encountered by many services sectors. As yet, trade in construction is not extensive and foreign revenues are generated by a small number of OECD firms. The current international construction market is smaller and more competitive than in earlier years due to declining demand from the developing countries, which account for over 60 per cent of OECD exports. Intra-OECD trade is the fastest growing market component and competition in construction services is expected to become more intense in the OECD area.

US firms maintain the largest world market share in construction services, although this share has diminished steadily in the 1980s due to decreased demand for large industrial projects and increased foreign competition. European construction firms have had the most remarkable showing in global markets in the 1980s and now account for over half of world exports of construction services. Italian firms, in particular, have gained a large share of the world construction market, and UK firms lead other European countries in exports of design engineering services. The Japanese have also steadily increased their share of world construction services exports.

The following are the major policy issues identified:

a) *Barriers to Trade in Services:* Trade in construction services is limited by non-tariff barriers in both OECD and non-OECD countries. Greater harmonization and liberalization of national policies affecting services through the OECD Codes of Liberalization and the GATT negotiations will enhance trade and fair competition in construction and other services sectors.

b) *Export Subsidies:* Export subsidies, in the form of interest rate subsidies on export financing and mixed credits, are distorting trade in construction and other services. OECD countries should continue to work together through the OECD Arrangement on Guidelines for Officially Supported Export Credits to agree on commercially realistic terms for export financing.

c) *Industrial Policies for Services:* There is growing recognition of the links between the competitiveness of manufacturing and services sectors and the need for governments to consider interrelated policy approaches. Industrial policymakers may want to give more attention to performance in services sectors and to factors such as services data, research, productivity, restructuring and global strategies.

II. INDUSTRY BACKGROUND

A. Industry Definition

Construction can be defined as the use of labour, materials and equipment to implement and complete a building project in accordance with approved plans and specifications. Construction is generally placed in a separate statistical category due to its mixture of manufacturing and non-manufacturing activities. Because it results in the output of a physical product, construction might be placed within the manufacturing sector. But construction is more often considered a process or service, and the trade problems that confront it are similar to those of other services sectors. For this reason, construction will be considered in this paper as a service industry.

The construction industry is a significant factor in the OECD economies, accounting for approximately 12 per cent of GDP in the OECD area compared to about 24 per cent for the manufacturing sector. In 1988, the OECD construction industry employed approximately 25 million persons accounting for 7 per cent of total employment in the OECD area. This includes both residential construction – private homes – and non-residential construction – manufacturing facilities, office and other commercial buildings, public works and infrastructure. Non-residential construction accounts for an estimated 58 per cent of total construction activity in the OECD countries. However, the non-residential share of total construction varies widely by country, ranging from almost 70 per cent of the total in Japan to 45 per cent in Italy in the 1980s.

This part focuses on the international construction industry, which in in the past has been mostly non-residential construction. Foreign activity in residential or private home construction is relatively smaller but growing. International construction projects tend to be large-scale and somewhat specialised, e.g., industrial facilities, chemical and other processing plants, transportation and communication systems, power generating plants, water and sewerage systems, and ports and airports.

The international construction industry itself can be divided into various types of services, primarily construction services and design engineering services. Construction services include scheduling and coordinating construction operations, procurement of materials, installation of equipment, supervision of labour and assigning tasks to subcontractors. Design engineering services include feasibility studies and the development of conceptual designs, project plans and engineering specifications. It is estimated that design engineering services account for 5 to 10 per cent of the total costs of a major construction project.

B.   Industry Structure

Like other services sectors, construction is primarily a domestic activity. While there are thousands of construction companies in the OECD countries, a small number of large firms generate most of the foreign revenues. The international construction industry is thus highly concentrated at the national level and relatively concentrated at the international level. In 1987, 25 multinational construction firms accounted for over 45 per cent of the global market as measured by the value of new international contract awards granted that year (see Table 30). While there are firms offering both construction and design engineering services, these activities are generally the domain of different companies. Table 31 shows the major international design engineering firms in 1987 as measured by their share of total international design billings. These data are derived from the annual survey of international construction and design engineering awards conducted by the journal *Engineering News Record* (ENR), which is a main source of statistics on this industry. Construction firms and design engineering firms are discussed separately below.

Table 30.   **Principal International Construction Firms: 1987**

	Company headquarters	Estimated foreign contracts signed (mil US$)	Total world market share[1] (%)
Davy Corp.	UK	3 519	4.4
Bechtel Group	US	3 315	4.2
M.W. Kellogg Co.	US	2 296	2.9
Philipp Holzmann	Germany	1 942	2.4
Bouygues	France	1 910	2.4
Dumez	France	1 731	2.2
SAE	France	1 696	2.1
Foster Wheeler	US	1 608	2.0
Parsons Corp.	US	1 558	1.9
Fiatimpresit	Italy	1 441	1.8
Mitsubishi	Japan	1 355	1.7
Kumagai Gumi	Japan	1 237	1.5
Brown & Root	US	1 190	1.5
Lummus	US	1 152	1.4
George Wimpey	UK	1 119	1.4
Saipem	Italy	1 088	1.4
Aoki Corp.	Japan	1 063	1.3
Fluor	US	1 047	1.3
Spie Batignolles	France	1 020	1.3
Bovis Intl.	UK	975	1.2
Bilfinger & Berger	Germany	924	1.2
Kaiser Engineers	US	817	1.0
Hochtief	Germany	810	1.0
Joannou	Cyprus	767	1.0
SGE Group	France	765	1.0
Total	25 firms	36 345	45.5

1. Market share based on total estimated foreign contracts market of $80 billion.
Source: Engineering News Record.

The United States construction industry is composed of more than 400 000 firms, but less than 0.1 per cent or about 400 companies are directly involved in international construction. In any given year, new contracts for foreign construction work will be gained by between 40 and 60 US firms. This group of multinationals is itself dominated by a few large construction companies who obtain 50 per cent or more of their revenues from foreign activities: M.W. Kellogg, Parsons, Bechtel, Foster Wheeler, Brown and Root, Lummus and Fluor. These firms have been among the top five or ten international contractors for most of the 1980s, although their ranking slipped slightly in 1987.

In the last five years, Japanese firms have emerged as strong competitors in the international construction industry. The Japanese construction sector, which is made up of over 500 000 enterprises, is dominated by six large firms: Shimizu, Taisei, Kajima, Takenaka, Ohbayashi and Kumagai Gumi. Kumagai Gumi has long been Japan's major international contractor with almost 50 per cent of its turnover derived from foreign work; Kajima and Shimizu have established subsidiaries in the United States and are increasing their construction exports to North America and Europe.

Europe's construction industry also consists of thousands of small firms and only a few larger companies competing in the international market. Davy Corp. of the United Kingdom was the top-ranked firm in 1987, displacing the US majors; other large UK international contractors include John Brown, Wimpey, Bovis and Balfour Beatty. France's firms – Bouygues, Dumez, Spie Batignolles, SAE and the SGE Group – have consistently ranked among the top international construction companies. In recent years, Italian firms have looked to overseas projects for a greater portion of revenues and increased their representation among the top international firms; they include Fiatimpresit, Saipem, Ansaldo and the Sadelmi Group. However, Italy's construction firms are much smaller than other European concerns; the largest firm Fiatimpresit ranks 39th in Europe in turns of turnover. Other top OECD contractors include Philipp Holzmann, Bilfinger & Berger Bau and Hochtief of Germany; Archirodon of Switzerland; Enka Inc. of Turkey; and PCL Construction of Canada.

Although the international construction industry has long been dominated by firms from the OECD countries, more companies from non-OECD countries are entering the market. Korean firms were major competitors in the 1970s and have consistently made a showing among the top contractors, although their rankings have declined since 1982. The major Korean construction firms include Daewoo, Hyundai, Daelim, Hanyang and Dong-Ah. Other non-OECD firms ranked among the top 100 in recent years include Joannou and Paraskevaides of Cyprus; Energopol of Poland; Larsen & Toubro of India; China State Construction of China; and Construtora Norberto of Brazil.

In the design engineering market, European design firms have generally improved their international rankings since 1982 at the expense of US and Canadian firms (see Table 31). In the United States, about 4 per cent of firms providing architectural, design and engineering services report foreign receipts; those with foreign sales generally get more than 20 per cent of their revenues overseas. The top-ranked US international design engineering firms include Morrison-Knudsen, Louis Berger, Metcalf & Eddy and Holmes & Narver. Canada's design firms, while relatively small in comparison with their foreign competitors, have generally been among the market leaders; they include the top-ranked Lavalin, the SNC Group, Monenco Ltd. and Golder Associates.

The Netherlands is home to several of Europe's top multinational design engineering firms, including Nedeco which has held the 4th or 5th place in the world for the last five years, Nethconsult, Fugro-McClelland and DHV Consulting. Other European firms among the top ten

Table 31. **Principal International Design Engineering Firms: 1987**

	Company headquarters	Type of firm	Estimated foreign sales (mil US$)
Lavalin Inc.	Canada	CE	> 50
Morrison-Knudsen	US	EA	> 50
Louis Berger	US	EAP	> 50
NEDECO	Netherlands	CE	> 50
Jaakko Poyry	Finland	CE	> 50
Nippon Koei	Japan	CE	> 50
SNC Group	Canada	CE	> 50
Metcalf & Eddy	US	EA	> 50
Nethconsult	Netherlands	CE	> 50
Dar Al-Handasah	Egypt	EAP	> 50
Tractebel	Belgium	CE	> 50
CDD	France	CE	> 50
Lahmeyer Intl.	Germany	CE	> 50
Electrowatt Eng.	Switzerland	CEA	> 50
Holmes & Narver	US	EA	> 50
Fugro-McClelland	Netherlands	SE	> 50
CRSS Inc.	US	EA	> 50
BCEOM	France	CE	> 50
Monenco Ltd.	Canada	CE	> 30
Pacific Consult.	Japan	CE	> 30
Ove Arup	UK	EA	> 30
Gibbs & Hill	US	EA	> 30
DHV Consulting	Netherlands	CE	> 30
Chas. T. Main	US	EA	> 30
Mott, Hay & Anderson	UK	CE	> 30
Total	25 firms		

CE = consulting engineer; EA = engineer-architect; P = planner; SE = soils or geotechnical engineer.
Source: Engineering News Record.

in recent years are Jaako Poyry of Finland, Tractebel of Belgium, CDD of France and Electrowatt Engineering of Switzerland. Major firms in the United Kingdom, which has traditionally been Europe's largest exporter of design engineering services, include Ove Arup, Mott, Hay & Anderson, Maunsell and Scott Wilson Kirkpatrick. Japanese design firms have not been as active as Japan's construction firms in the international market, although Nippon Koei and Pacific Consultants have been among the leading world firms for the last five years. The mid-1980s have been marked by the entry of a number of new firms to the international design market including those from Egypt, Brazil, Korea, Taiwan, India, Yugoslavia and Hungary.

C. Demand Trends

Demand for international construction has slowed and shifted from the non-OECD countries to the OECD countries in the 1980s. As a result, the current international construction market is smaller and more competitive than in earlier years. The worldwide recession in the early 1980s, declining oil prices and growing debt problems have limited the ability of many

Table 32. **Regional Trends in International Construction Awards**

Percentages[1]

	International Construction		International Design	
	1983	1987	1983	1987
Middle East	35.2	18.1	34.8	18.5
Africa	22.9	12.2	21.2	23.6
Asia	16.5	20.9	21.4	28.2
Europe	10.2	23.3	10.3	13.2
North America	8.5	15.5	2.6	5.7
Latin America	6.7	10.0	9.7	10.8
Total	100.0	100.0	100.0	100.0
Total (bil US$)	93.6	73.9	3.9	4.0

1. Share of total in current US$. Based on awards to top 250 construction firms and billings by top 200 design firms.
Source: Engineering News Record.

non-OECD countries to finance new construction projects; these countries are also granting a larger share of construction work to indigenous firms. According to the ENR survey, the dollar volume of new international construction awards has declined steadily since the 1981 peak of nearly $130 billion, while the value of new design billings has increased only slightly (see Table 32). The Middle East, Africa and Latin America, which traditionally accounted for over 65 per cent of new construction and design engineering awards to foreign firms, accounted for 40 per cent of the construction market and 53 per cent of the design market in 1987.

The Middle Eastern countries were the largest single market for construction services during the 1970s and early 1980s, but demand has fallen markedly since 1983 due to declining real oil prices and substantial cutbacks in major projects in the energy-producing countries. In Africa and Latin America, debt burdens and difficulty in obtaining outside financing have constrained the growth of construction projects. Most new projects in the non-OECD countries are also smaller in scale than those of earlier years due to world industrial overcapacity and previous infrastructure development. There have been less dramatic declines in the design market in non-OECD areas due to its smaller scale and the continuing need to import technically demanding engineering services.

Growth in OECD demand for non-residential construction has varied by region in the 1980s. Overall, real growth in investment in non-residential construction in the OECD countries after 1973 was low or negative compared to the 5 to 6 per cent annual growth experienced in the 1960s and early 1970s. Investment in non-residential construction picked up again in the OECD area in 1984 (see Table 33). The North American construction market showed strong growth in 1984-85, but this commercial building boom then peaked resulting in excess capacity in non-residential structures and industrial facilities. The trade deficit in the United States has also reduced the need for new manufacturing plants. The US Department of Commerce predicts that commercial construction in the United States may continue to decline in the short-term with business investment weighted toward new equipment rather than structures. Demand for non-residential construction in both the United States and Canada is expected to be somewhat depressed through 1989.

Table 33.   **Real Growth in Investment in Non-Residential Construction**[1]

Percentages

	1984	1985	1986	1987
North America				
United States	10.0	5.4	–5.5	–1.3
Canada	–1.4	8.0	–6.6	–2.0
Japan	–0.5	0.1	4.4	6.0[2]
EEC Europe	1.3	0.3	4.4	5.4
Germany	1.1	–1.1	5.7	1.4
France	–1.7	0.8	5.5	5.4
United Kingdom	9.9	–1.0	1.3	5.3
Italy	0.5	1.9	0.9	1.4
Spain	–4.1	3.8	9.4	6.7[2]
Australia	4.9	9.2	3.6	3.0[2]
Total OECD	3.3	2.1	1.8	2.3[2]

1. Annual percentage increase in constant prices.
2. Estimates.
Source: OECD National Accounts.

European non-residential construction demand has followed an opposite pattern, experiencing low growth through 1985 and a boom since 1986. Europe was the largest market for international construction contracts in 1987 as measured by the ENR survey. Since 1986, the United Kingdom and Spain have registered the highest growth in investment in non-residential construction among the European countries. Real growth in investment in commercial and industrial construction has also been steady in Germany, Italy, France and the Netherlands. In 1988, investment in non-residential construction in Europe reached record levels and growth in demand is expected to persist through 1989 although at a lower rate.

Japan, which maintains the highest ratio of construction investment to GDP of the OECD countries, has also experienced rapid growth in non-residential construction demand in the mid-1980s due partly to government policies to expand domestic consumption. In 1987, Japan exceeded the United States in construction investment for the first time to become the world's largest non-residential construction market due mainly to the rapid and steep rise in the yen rate afer the Plaza Accord of September 1985. Redevelopment plans spurred by rising urban land prices and increased investment by Japan's manufacturing sector in new facilities have contributed to Japan's building boom. A number of major construction projects are planned or underway including airports, bridges and urban redevelopment projects. Japan's investment in public works projects and other non-residential construction sectors is expected to remain at a high rate through 1989.

D. Production and Trade Trends

The OECD countries account for over 90 per cent of world exports of construction and design engineering services, with about 70 per cent of these exports destined for non-OECD countries. Intra-OECD trade has increased from 20 per cent to 30 per cent of total trade since l983 and is the fastest growing component. But trade in construction services, as in other services sectors, is small compared to trade in manufactured goods. The value of foreign construction contracts in relation to domestic non-residential construction output is relatively low for most countries, as is the rate of import penetration or domestic work gained by foreign contractors (see Table 34). Still, construction is one of the most traded services in the international market, together with transportation, travel, financial and professional services and licensing. The trade statistics presented here should be interpreted with caution due to difficulties in measuring imports and exports in construction as in other services sectors. In construction services, the tendency of firms to create a network of autonomous operating companies in different localities around the world could mask the full extent of trade in this sector.

Table 34.   **Production and Trade in Non-Residential Construction: 1987**

	Value of Output (mil US$)	Export Shares[1] (%)	Import Penetration[2] (%)
United States	202 000	9.0	4.4
Canada	26 000	6.9	10.0
Japan	283 000	3.5	0.8
Europe[3]	220 000	18.0	7.0
Germany	50 800	11.6	4.5
France	31 200	27.6	1.7
United Kingdom	23 600	33.5	n.a.
Italy	21 500	43.8	n.a.
Austria	8 200	6.4	3.9
Belgium	6 300	7.5	4.8
Denmark	6 700	2.0	n.a.
Finland	5 900	1.6	5.3
Greece	2 500	6.4	n.a.
Netherlands	6 800	20.6	1.5
Norway	6 700	4.5	4.5
Portugal	2 300	2.6	n.a.
Spain	22 300	1.7	9.6
Sweden	9 300	12.9	8.6
Switzerland	9 700	12.4	n.a.
Turkey	4 200	19.0	n.a.
Australia	11 400	2.1	20.8
New Zealand	2 200	8.7	20.0
Total	745 000		

n.a. = not available.
1. Export Shares – value of foreign contracts won by domestic firms as share of domestic output.
2. Import Penetration – value of domestic contracts won by foreign firms as share of domestic output.
3. Includes intra-European trade.
Source: OECD estimates.

Exports of construction services by US firms have declined as a share of construction output since the early l980s largely because a shrinking international market and decreased demand for large industrial projects have led American firms to concentrate more on domestic work. Other factors contributing to a reduced US presence in international construction include concern about payment delays or default and increased foreign competition. At the same time, foreign contractors have been gaining a larger share of the US market, although this is still relatively low. Many of the larger OECD contractors have entered the US market in recent years due to declining prospects in non-OECD countries; this has led to some decrease in the US trade surplus in construction services.

Japan's construction industry, now the world's largest, has had the least trade exposure of the OECD countries. Japan's top multinationals have maintained a steady level of foreign construction contracts during the l980s, but these have accounted for a decreasing share of total turnover or less than 4 per cent in l987. Import penetration in Japan is among the lowest in the OECD countries. However, Japan's trade in construction services is expected to increase as Japanese construction companies follow manufacturing and financial firms overseas and foreign firms demand greater access to the domestic construction market.

The European countries have the highest share of construction exports in relation to total turnover whether or not intra-European trade is included. The overall import penetration rate drops to less than 4 per cent when intra-European trade is excluded, indicating Europe's large trade surplus in construction services with the rest of the world. Italy's construction firms now engage in overseas work for almost half the value of domestic turnover, while the industries of the United Kingdom, France and the Netherlands also show a marked export orientation. Turkey's construction industry has steadily increased its foreign work; the firms of Turkey, Switzerland and Italy have traditionally been among the most dependent on foreign work in the ENR survey of the top 250 firms. Canada, Australia and New Zealand are among the OECD countries showing a trade deficit in construction services; Japanese firms have recently won large infrastructure contracts in the Australian market.

Overall OECD trade in design engineering services is less extensive than trade in construction services (see Table 35). In the United States, design engineering firms are estimated to carry out over 95 per cent of their activities in their home market with many firms reducing their dependence on foreign work in recent years. Foreign design firms have captured less than 1 per cent of the extensive US market with Canadian companies accounting for the largest portion. In the mid-l980s, the United States is estimated to be running a trade surplus of about $1 billion per year in design engineering services. Canada's strong design engineering sector maintains a sizeable trade surplus, with US work accounting for about 30 per cent of the total. Japan's design services firms, like Japanese construction firms, have had the least exposure to international competition.

The American market for design engineering services is some four times larger than the European market where public in-house engineering reduces demand for the services of private firms. As a result, European design engineering firms carry out about a third of their activities in foreign markets. The largest exporter of these design services in absolute terms is the United Kingdom whose top 25 multinationals traditionally account for a quarter of European exports. German, French and Dutch firms also depend on foreign billings for about a third of revenues, while Italian firms have the highest export shares and have been gaining importance in international design markets. Other significant European exporters of design engineering services are Switzerland, Finland, Denmark, Sweden and Belgium. European imports of design engineering services, which are mostly intra-EC market exchanges, do not exceed 5 per cent of total turnover.

Table 35. **Production and Trade in Design Engineering: 1987**

	Value of Output (mil US$)	Export Shares[1] (%)	Import Penetration[2] (%)
United States	46 000	3.5	0.5
Japan	22 000	1.2	0.1
Europe[3]	11 000	32.0	4.8
Germany	1 800	34.0	
France	1 850	32.0	
United Kingdom	3 500	33.0	
Italy	1 200	50.0	
Netherlands	500	25.0	
Canada	4 000	13.0	0.6
Australia	1 400	2.1	n.a.
Total	84 400		

1. Export Shares – value of foreign billings won by domestic firms as share of domestic output.
2. Import Penetration – value of domestic billings won by foreign firms as share of domestic output.
3. Includes intra-European trade.
Source: OECD estimates.

As seen in the evolution of world market shares in the ENR survey, US firms have the largest market share in both construction and design engineering services although this share has diminished steadily in the 1980s (see Table 36). Between 1982 and 1987, US firms lost market share in international construction to European and Japanese companies and in design engineering to Canadian, Japanese and non-OECD firms. Japanese firms have increased their market share in construction in this period to rank second behind the United States, while their share of the design services market has more than doubled but remains relatively small.

European construction firms have had the most remarkable showing in global markets in the 1980s and now account for over half of world exports of construction services. Italian firms have steadily increased their representation and have accounted for the largest share of European construction exports since 1983. Firms from France and the United Kingdom have also increased their market shares in this period. Turkish firms, which have served as primary contractors for a large number of civil works projects in the Middle East, have maintained a 2 to 3 per cent share of world construction exports during the 1980s although this fell in 1987. In design engineering services, European firms have maintained but not increased their world market share. The United Kingdom continues to be the European market leader in the export of design services, with Germany, French and Dutch firms interchanging the next three positions in any given year.

Construction awards to Korean firms peaked in 1982, when Korea ranked second with over 11 per cent of world exports of construction services as measured by the ENR survey. Korean construction exports rose from $83 million in 1972 to $8 billion in 1978 peaking at $14 billion in 1981 due partly to a competitive advantage in low labour costs. However, this advantage was largely negated by rising wage rates and the higher cost of transporting Korean workers

Table 36.   **Trends in International Market Shares**[1]

Percentages

Firm Headquarters	International Construction		International Design	
	1982	1987	1982	1987
United States	36.5	24.5	33.8	25.9
Canada	0.3	0.6	7.8	12.9
Japan	7.6	13.4	3.0	6.4
Europe	37.7	53.7	48.1	48.4
France	9.3	11.6	8.7	6.5
Germany	7.7	8.0	6.1	8.9
Italy	6.3	12.4	0.8	1.7
United Kingdom	6.1	10.7	13.8	11.2
Netherlands	1.6	1.9	4.5	8.9
Switzerland	0.3	1.6	3.7	2.8
Scandanavian	0.7	2.0	7.4	5.1
Other	5.7	5.5	3.1	3.2
Turkey	2.2	1.1	0.0	0.0
Korea	11.2	2.8	0.9	1.7
All Other	4.5	4.5	6.4	4.7
Total	100.0	100.0	100.0	100.0
Total (bil US$)	123.1	73.9	3.7	4.0

1. Based on contracts awarded to top 250 construction firms and billings by top 200 design firms.
Source: Engineering News Record.

overseas. In addition, the decline in Middle East demand for infrastructure construction, the traditional Korean market focus, was a major contributor to Korea's loss of market share. No other non-OECD country has reached a position in international construction or design engineering services commensurate with that of Korea, although several non-OECD firms rank among the top.

The regional division of construction and design work as measured by the ENR survey can be seen in Tables 37 and 38. European construction and design firms dominate in all markets but particularly in Africa. The African construction market has traditionally been served by French and British firms due partly to colonial ties. However, in the past few years, Italian firms have held the largest share of the African construction market; Africa accounted for over a quarter of contract awards to Italian firms in 1986 and 1987. The African design market continues to be the domain of French firms, who have generally held the largest market share. The US market share in African construction awards has declined by half since 1982, although US and Canadian firms continue to gain a significant share of the design billings.

European and American firms continue to vie for the dwindling Middle East construction and design market, where Saudi Arabia is the largest importer of such services. The Middle East remains the greatest single source of construction awards for US firms, although many large-scale oil-related projects are now being scaled down or postponed. In recent years, American firms have faced increasing competition in the Middle East market from Italian, Korean and Turkish contractors. The Middle East design services market has long been

Table 37. **Regional Market Shares in Construction: 1987**[1]

Percentages

	Firm Headquarters:					Total
	Europe	US	Japan	Korea	Other	
Europe	57.6	29.9	9.3	0.0	3.2	100.0
North America	65.8	9.1	19.8	0.04	5.3	100.0
Asia	39.4	22.7	28.8	2.4	6.7	100.0
Middle East	41.1	38.1	5.4	12.0	3.4	100.0
Africa	87.4	7.2	2.1	1.2	2.1	100.0
Latin America	48.7	35.7	9.3	0.07	6.3	100.0

1. Based on contracts awarded to top 250 international firms.
Source: Engineering News Record.

dominated by US and British firms due to their expertise in industrial and processing plant projects, although the US share has declined in the 1980s.

Japanese construction and design firms have made their best showing in the Asian market, which accounts for about half of Japanese construction and design services exports. In 1987, China was Asia's largest construction market followed by Indonesia, Thailand, Malaysia and the Phillipines. US firms have lost considerable market share in Asia primarily to British contractors and design firms. In contrast, US construction and design firms have maintained their market share in the Latin American market. Italian contractors have been strong competition in the Latin American construction market with over a 25 per cent share in recent years, and Canadian and French firms are important exporters of design services to Latin America. In both Asia and Latin America, local companies are beginning to take a larger share of domestic contracts.

European firms, primarily German, have been the main exporters of construction services to the large North American market, although Japanese firms have more than doubled their

Table 38. **Regional Market Shares in Design Services: 1987**[1]

Percentages

	Firm Headquarters						Total
	Europe	US	Canada	Japan	Korea	Other	
Europe	48.4	25.9	12.9	6.4	1.7	4.7	100.0
North America	29.2	8.0	53.2	0.4	0.5	8.7	100.0
Asia	45.5	21.2	9.3	16.8	3.8	3.4	100.0
Middle East	49.8	32.1	1.9	2.7	2.8	10.7	100.0
Africa	68.2	15.7	10.0	2.3	0.3	3.5	100.0
Latin America	27.7	55.3	9.1	5.4	0.0	2.5	100.0

1. Based on billings by top 200 international firms.
Source: Engineering News Record.

market share since 1984. Much of the European penetration can be attributed to buyouts of US construction firms; the ENR survey counts these firms' US contracts as part of the parents' total. Much of the Japanese increase is due to foreign investment in real estate development and manufacturing facilities in the United States. Canadian firms lead other foreign competitors in the US design market accounting for 60 per cent of US imports of design services in 1987. Among the European design firms operating in North America, Dutch and Swiss firms have accounted for the largest market share in recent years. Many European design firms have established footholds in the US market by buying portions of large American firms.

European firms dominate the European construction and design markets which are characterised by intra-European trade in these services. This market also includes exports to East Europe and the Soviet Union, primarily the domain of European firms. US firms are important exporters of construction and design services to Europe, although their share of new construction contracts has decreased since the early 1980s. The US position in the European international design market has been strongly challenged by Scandanavian and Canadian firms. In addition, Japanese firms have been looking to the growing European market to expand their construction services exports and have recently won contracts in the United Kingdom and Spain. More than half of the Japanese contractors in the ENR survey reported winning new work in Europe in 1987. It is expected that foreign construction work in Europe will increase as foreign firms establish commercial and manufacturing facilities there prior to 1992.

III. MAJOR COMPETITIVE FACTORS

A. Costs

Costs and prices are major competitive factors in the international construction industry due to the use of a bid and tender system which is common in many service industries. In their bid for a particular project, contractors generally offer a comprehensive price which reflects total costs and the desired return. Many factors may contribute to the ability of firms to undercut their competitors on price, including lower labour costs, superior labour productivity, lower materials costs, lower transportation costs for equipment and personnel, less costly financing and/or willingness to accept a lower rate of return.

Labour costs are the most important cost consideration in international construction projects, which are generally labour-intensive infrastructure or industrial ventures. Large wage differentials between OECD and non-OECD countries have acted to the detriment of OECD construction firms, particularly in the 1970s and early 1980s. Firms from non-OECD countries are able to undercut on projects requiring little technical expertise but a high input of semi-skilled and unskilled labour and often export construction teams from their home countries to take advantage of low wage rates. In this way, Korean firms captured a large share of the Middle East construction market in the 1970s; newer competitors from Brazil, Yugoslavia, India and Taiwan are now winning bids on the basis of low labour costs. Turkey also has a large low-wage labour sector which has benefitted its firms in bidding on Middle East projects. In general, OECD firms use local labour and often subcontract labour-intensive portions of projects to local firms or subsidiaries in order to cut costs. OECD construction firms are more successful in competing for projects in non-OECD countries when the projects are technically demanding or where they can offer attractive financial packages.

Labour productivity increases in the OECD construction sector have been slow due to the cyclical nature of demand, the absence of standardisation and a relatively low level of research and development. As in some other services sectors, labour productivity growth in construction has lagged behind that in manufacturing and agriculture. However, it should be noted that there are conceptual and operational difficulties in measuring productivity in services sectors such as construction. It is estimated that labour productivity in the OECD construction sector grew at a rate of less than 1.0 per cent per year in the period 1979 to 1986 compared to 3.5 per cent in manufacturing and 4.4 per cent in agriculture. In both the United States and Europe, productivity in the construction industry has changed little since the 1960s. Productivity growth has been higher in international construction than in domestic residential construction sectors, but still remains below that in manufacturing. Scope remains for improving labour productivity and offsetting high OECD wage costs through automation of construction processes and more offsite prefabrication, both areas where Japanese contractors have been the technical leaders.

The profitability of many international construction projects is eroding in the current competitive market as firms accept lower rates of return to win projects and to break into new markets, particularly in other OECD countries. The US Department of Commerce has predicted that foreign contractors in the United States will not gain more than 10 per cent of the domestic construction market in the 1990s due to their heavy losses on current projects. According to the ENR survey, only 84 per cent of the top construction companies reported making a profit on their foreign work in 1987 with the median profit margin slipping from 4.4 per cent in 1986 to 4.0 per cent. In the past, European contractors have reported the highest profits on foreign work according to ENR.

B. Financing

The provision of project financing may be the single most important factor in the competitiveness of the OECD construction industry in bidding on projects in the developing countries, which account for 60 per cent or more of OECD exports. In order to win contracts, construction firms must often put together a financing package for the client through arrangements with commercial banks or their own governments. Few developing countries can assemble the necessary financial packages for large construction projects and commonly ask foreign contractors to submit financing proposals along with bids. Construction firms which can provide financing on favourable terms and conditions thus receive a competitive edge. According to the 1987 ENR survey, 57 per cent of respondents bid for contracts that required them to arrange major financing and 54 per cent of these firms won their bids. The main sources of this financing were commercial bank loans and government funds; countertrade and equity financing are also used but are of lesser importance.

Countries with large and progressive banking sectors have an advantage in providing project financing for international construction bids. Firms from the United Kingom and the United States benefit from their extensive international banking sectors, while construction firms from France and Japan derive advantage from the close coordination between their financial and construction sectors. Construction industries in other countries now recognise the need to gain a better grasp of the financing aspects of international bidding and to develop creative financing packages and closer relationships with domestic banks.

The role of OECD governments in construction project financing has also been extensive. Most OECD governments provide export credits to the construction industry which allow the foreign buyer of the exported construction services and goods to defer payment. This may include guarantees or insurance to cover default of payment to the exporter and export financing. The level and types of financing, interest rates and institutional arrangements for providing export credits vary greatly by country. Some governments also extend mixed credits to the construction industry which combine export financing with official development assistance in the form of low-interest loans. Most OECD governments participate in the OECD Arrangement on Guidelines for Officially Supported Export Credits, which sets basic rules for the provision of export credits and also mixed credits.

OECD governments also use tied aid in support of their construction industries; loans and grants to developing countries for specific infrastructure, utility or other construction projects are often tied to procurement of goods and services in the donor country. In 1987, almost $9 billion in aid was provided by the OECD Development Assistance Committee (DAC) Member countries for construction projects in the developing countries or about 29 per cent of total bilateral aid (see Table 39). Over 60 per cent of construction aid was tied to purchases in

Table 39. **Development Aid Flows for Construction Projects: 1987**

	Bilateral Aid[1] (mil US$)	Of which Tied Aid[2] (%)	Associated Financing (mil US$)	Of which AF-ODA (%)
Australia	24.0	78	3.0	3
Canada	262.0	65	32.0	4
Denmark	123.0	47	0.0	0
Finland	99.0	89	0.0	0
France	600.0	93	119.0	7
Germany	1 133.0	49	0.0	0
Italy	1 160.0	66	583.0	24
Japan	3 360.0	53	57.0	0
Netherlands	486.0	51	120.0	11
Norway	142.0	54	0.0	0
Sweden	141.0	6	81.0	19
Switzerland	76.0	32	27.0	12
United Kingdom	180.0	64	161.0	29
United States	851.0	100	0.0	0
Total	8 640.0	63	1 181.0	5

AF = Associated Financing. ODA = Official Development Assistance.
1. May overstate aid in including some unrelated equipment.
2. Includes partially untied aid. Excludes ODA in associated financing.
Source: OECD Creditor Reporting System.

the donor country compared to a 50 per cent ratio of tied aid for total bilateral assistance; this includes partially untied aid which allows for purchases in developing countries. In addition, more than $1 billion in associated financing, including mixed credits, was extended to construction projects in the developing countries; this accounted for more than half of total associated financing by the DAC countries in 1987.

The competitiveness of construction firms in non-OECD foreign markets is thus affected by the attitude of their governments towards development assistance, tied aid and associated financing. Some countries (e.g., the United States, Australia, Austria, Belgium) give a small share or no development aid for construction projects, while in other countries (e.g., Japan, Italy) construction aid accounts for a relatively large share of total bilateral aid. Most OECD countries tie this foreign aid to the purchase of construction services in their country. Finland, France and the United States are among those countries which tend to tie most or all of this aid, while countries such as Sweden leave most construction aid untied. The large share of African construction awards to Italian firms in 1987 is partly due to an extensive government aid programme in that year, a large share of which was tied aid. Some countries, such as France, Italy, the Netherlands, Sweden and the United Kingdom, make relatively greater use of associated financing including mixed credits in financing construction projects in developing countries. The aid included in these financial packages is usually tied to procurement in the donor country. The role of governments in putting together project financing, particularly export financing subsidised through low interest rates or mixed credits, is a controversial aspect of international construction trade.

C. Technology

The technical qualifications of construction and design engineering firms are an important competitive factor in the bidding process. The international construction industry is somewhat specialised with firms being strongest in technologies important in their home market. US firms are leaders in offshore drilling technologies and power and process plant construction; French firms in nuclear power plant construction; Japanese firms in high-speed railroads, underground construction, seismic design and bridge construction; German firms in concrete construction; and Swiss and Austrian firms in ground stabilisation techniques and tunneling technology.

European and Japanese construction firms have emerged as the leaders in developing innovative construction methods and related specialised equipment. Their competitive strategies are based on establishing proprietary positions in their technical specialities and using this expertise to enter new markets and increase earnings through licensing. The strength of US firms is in complex engineering technologies and project management rather than in construction methods. US firms have maintained an edge in the design of industrial processing plants, such as petrochemicals and utilities, and in managing construction of large and complex projects. Non-OECD firms generally rely on joint ventures and other arrangements with OECD firms in bidding on technology-intensive construction projects.

US firms maintain a clear lead is the application of computers to construction management and design engineering. US companies have developed software packages and onsite computer systems for project scheduling, cost accounting, materials tracking and organisation of subcontractors. Components can be coded and tracked from the design phase through fabrication, delivery, construction and inspection. Such management systems, which are not in widespread use outside of the United States, allow significant gains in efficiency and productivity. US firms also use computer-assisted methods for design engineering and integrate these with management databases to reduce costs. The application of computer techniques has assisted US design firms in maintaining market share, but cost savings from computer applications have been generally insufficient to counter the US disadvantage in labour costs in many construction bids.

European and Japanese firms are leaders in applying computers to construction methods and in automating construction processes. Japanese companies have invested heavily in the development of automated construction equipment to reduce manpower requirements, improve productivity and handle hazardous jobs. They have developed computer-aided construction processes for earthmoving, tunneling, steel fabrication and pouring and spreading concrete and are attempting to develop robots for specified construction tasks. European firms are working to automate the highly labour-intensive tasks of cutting, bending and placing reinforcing bars and cables. Innovations in many construction materials, including new engineering materials and synthetic fibers, have originated in Europe and Japan. European firms lead in sophisticated concrete techniques, including slipform construction for high-rise buildings and onsite precasting of concrete. Japanese firms are developing a specialty in construction of prefabricated modules, including offshore drilling platforms and piping and wiring systems, which can be transported to distant construction sites.

Overall R&D intensity in the construction industry is very low with R&D expenditures averaging less than 0.1 per cent of net industry output in most countries (see Table 40). In the case of the larger multinationals, it is estimated that US firms spend less than 1.0 per cent of gross receipts on research and development, compared to nearly 3 per cent for Japanese and European companies. Japanese and European firms spend heavily on research on basic construction methods, with the larger companies maintaining substantial R&D programs and in-

Table 40. **R&D Expenditures and Researchers in the Construction Industry: 1985**

	Business Researchers	R&D Expenditures (mil US$)
Australia	90	8.2
Austria	17	2.3
Belgium	n.a.	11.2
Denmark	16	5.1
France	399	57.6
Germany	411	63.8
Italy	87	16.5
Japan	5 752	493.5
Netherlands	130	16.9
Spain	139	18.8
United Kingdom	200	37.6
United States	n.a.	54.0

n.a. = not vailable.
Source: OECD Science, Technology and Industrial Indicators Division.

house laboratories. US research is more concentrated on process design, systems control and advanced computer applications. US firms seldom operate their own R&D laboratories or invest heavily in the development of proprietary construction technologies; most US R&D takes place outside the industry – in universities, government laboratories, equipment and materials firms and clients such as utility companies. In general, US construction firms have sought the position of technology broker or service provider rather than technology originator in regard to construction methods; some believe that underinvestment in new construction technologies may place the US industry at a disadvantage relative to other OECD firms in the long-run.

D. Packaging

The ability to provide a total services package is becoming a more important competitive factor in the international construction market. Public authorities and private clients are now looking to firms to provide a complete construction package, including design engineering, construction and management services as well as project financing. As a result, the distinction between contractors, architects, consulting engineers and other construction professionals is becoming blurred as firms diversify to new areas. Many believe the future of international construction lies with fewer, larger firms providing a broader range of technical, management as well as financial services.

The two most common forms of contracts are design-bid-build, where design and construction are awarded under different contracts, and design-construct, where one contract is awarded. According to the ENR survey, design-construct contracts are becoming more common accounting for 26 per cent of total foreign construction contracts in 1987. As shown in Table 41, US firms have been losing their predominance in this type of combined contract, their share of total design-construct contracts dropping from 43 per cent to 19 per cent between 1982

Table 41. **Market Shares in Design-Construct Contracts**[1]

Percentages

	1982	1987
United States	43.0	19.0
Japan	21.0	18.0
Europe	31.0	55.0
Germany	7.0	3.0
France	18.0	22.0
United Kingdom	1.0	5.0
Italy	1.0	22.0
Turkey	4.0	0.0
Korea	5.0	2.0
Other	0.0	6.0
Total	100.0	100.0

1. Based on value of design-construct contracts of top firms.
Source: Engineering News Record.

and 1987. Design-construct contracts as a share of total construction contracts awarded to US firms have decreased from 65 per cent to 23 per cent in this period. This is largely due to declining demand for the type of large-scale design-construct work performed by US firms invoving petroleum, petrochemical, utility and other industrial plants. While many US firms are integrated service providers, they have not succeeded in adapting these skills to the smaller-scale, conventional infrastructure-type projects now in growing demand.

Construction firms from France and Italy are having the most success in bidding on design-construct work overseas, partly because their integrated firms offer complete design and construction packages for smaller-scale projects. These firms provide a full range of engineering and construction services, from basic design through scheduling and coordination of construction activities, procurement of materials, equipment and subcontractors and personnel training. In addition, bidding procedures in these countries, which often require firms to submit proposals covering design and construction as well as evaluation of alternative construction techniques, are conducive to promoting a diversity of expertise. French and Italian firms also benefit from their membership in large industrial and financial groups in the private and public sectors which can provide financing assistance.

Japanese firms have made a consistent showing in their share of international design-construct contracts largely by winning several smaller contracts. As in other Japanese industrial sectors, construction firms bidding on foreign work are often part of larger integrated companies or have links to related firms. Design and construction firms may cooperate in bidding jointly on foreign design-construct projects. Japanese construction firms also have close links with their subcontractors, who are often captive companies, and are particularly deft at integrating scheduling, delivery and other management services.

OECD countries with more specialist contractors may find themselves at a disadvantage in future international construction competition. Firms from the United Kingdom and Germany have not fared as well in packaging design and construction services. In the United Kingdom, in particular, the independent consultant is more common than the integrated contracting firm which can provide the complete design and build or turnkey project. Canadian and Dutch firms are strong in design engineering but not as highly ranked in international construction. Turkey's construction firms are competitive in lower-skill infrastructure projects such as harbours, dams and roads, but Turkish design firms are not fully experienced in engineering for more sophisticated projects. In the future, the success of many international contractors may depend on their ability to combine design and construction and diversify their services packages whether through restructuring, acquisitions or joint ventures with foreign partners.

IV. INDUSTRIAL AND TRADE POLICIES

Specific government industrial and trade policies for the international construction industry are rare among the OECD countries. However, the economic policies pursued by governments affect the construction industry indirectly through exchange rates, interest rates and the rate of inflation. In addition, the international construction industry is affected by government treatment of foreign activities and income earned abroad as well as by export financing systems (see Table 42).

Corporate and personal taxation of overseas earnings affects the overall profits of construction firms and their ability to offer lower bids. US firms are at the greatest disadvantage in this regard, although a number of other countries have a partial tax on corporate earnings abroad. Firms from countries other than the United States and Japan benefit from a rebate on value-added tax on exported materials and services. Grants and loans for feasibility studies for foreign projects are available in most countries as is insurance to reduce credit, political and exchange rate risks. Many governments provide bid and performance bonds, which are often required by clients to ensure the seriousness of bids and the quality of completed work. The United States maintains Corrupt Practices and Anti-Boycott Acts designed to prevent bribery and discrimination in overseas markets; such legislation can be a competitive disadvantage to firms. Many countries encourage or support joint ventures and consortia of construction firms, particularly small and medium-sized companies, in competing for international projects.

A. United States

Specific US Government support for the construction industry is mostly for research and development, primarily funded by the Department of Defense. In 1986, about $270 million was spent on military-related construction R&D, primarily the water and port projects of the Army Corps of Engineers. Non-military government research spending on construction is estimated at less than $30 million per year, mainly through the Center for Building Technology of the National Bureau of Standards (NBS), the National Science Foundation university grants and the Federal Highway Administration. Recently, the US government through the Department of Defense funded two university Centers of Excellence on Advanced Contruction Technology and initiated a joint government-industry project on Construction Productivity Advancement Research (CPAR). These programmes are intended to increase investment in construction research and promote the transfer of construction technology developed in federal and university laboratories to the private sector.

Government policies affecting US construction firms in foreign markets may be more disadvantageous than in other countries, as US firms are more heavily taxed and subject to anti-

Table 42. **Government Policies Affecting the Construction Industry**

	US	Japan	UK	Germany	France	Italy	Korea
Tax on Personal Income Abroad	Yes	No	No	No	No	No	No
Tax on Corporate Income Abroad	Yes	No	Lim.	Lim.	Lim.	No	Lim
Rebate VAT on exported goods and services	Lim.	Lim.	Yes	Yes	Yes	Yes	Yes
Grants and loans for feasibility studies	Yes	Lim.	Yes	Lim.	Yes	Yes	Yes
Export Credit Insurance	Yes	Lim.	Yes	Yes	Yes	Yes	Yes
Exchange Rate Insurance	No	No	Yes	Yes	Yes	Yes	No
Political Risk Insurance	Yes	Yes	Yes	Yes	Yes	Yes	Yes
Bid and performance bonds and guarantees	No	Yes	Yes	Yes	Yes	Yes	No
Corrupt Practices Act	Yes	No	No	No	No	No	No
Anti-Boycott Act	Yes	No	No	No	No	No	No
Encourages consortia for foreign projects	No	No	Yes	No	Yes	Yes	Yes

Lim. = Limited.
Source: Engineering News Record.

boycott, anti-bribery and anti-trust rules. In regard to export assistance, the Export-Import Bank (Eximbank) is the main government-funded source of loans, guarantees and other types of export financing for construction firms. The Eximbank provides direct loans at OECD consensus rates, guarantees commercial bank loans and provides credit risk protection to support US exports, including construction services. The Eximbank also supports the Engineer Multiplier Program, which provides medium-term financing for feasibility studies and pre-construction design-engineering services, specifically intended to assist US architectural and engineering firms win foreign contracts.

In 1983, the US Congress established an associated financing programme as part of the Eximbank's charter in order to counter mixed credits being extended by other governments to construction and other industries. The Tied Aid Credit Program, jointly adminstered by the Eximbank and the Agency for International Development, provides development aid and export credits tied to US procurement and is aimed at supporting firms in matching situations where competitors are financed by foreign governments. Funding for this programme, which is viewed as a defensive weapon, was increased by $300 million in 1986-87. As yet, the US construction industry has taken little advantage of this programme. Other construction support is provided by the Trade and Development Program, which gives grants for feasibility studies and consultancy services in developing countries, particularly for large public sector projects.

The US Government consulted with the Japanese Government concerning increased access for US firms to Japan's construction market, particularly for public works projects. In May 1988, the Japanese Government notified the US Government of special measures on 17 public works project involving $18 billion of potential work. These special measures are intended to provide sufficient expanded opportunities to foreign companies so that they may become familiar with the public works bidding system. At least seven joint ventures between US and Japanese firms have been formed for Japanese public project competitions since the agreement was signed. Under provisions of the Omnibus Trade and Competitiveness Act of

1988, the US government is now studying the openness of Japan's contract award system and other practices with respect to imports of US engineering and construction services. In addition, the FY 1988 Budget Appropriations Act had prohibited the awarding of federally-funded public works contracts to contractors from Japan because Japan excluded American contractors from public works projects.

B. Japan

In 1986, the Construction Industry Council published *Visions of the Construction Industry toward the 21st Century* which recommended that the Japanese construction industry undertake efforts to improve the soundness of the management of construction copanies and eliminate structural problems in the industry. The private sector funds the bulk of construction research and development in Japan, although the government coordinates cooperative research projects among firms; Japan has the highest level of R&D spending in the construction sector.

The Japanese Government maintains an export credit system which is in accordance with the OECD Arrangement on export credits. Regarding the government's large bilateral aid programme administered by the Overseas Economic Cooperation Fund (OECF), the government has announced its intention to further increase the level of untied aid in its bilateral assistance programmes.

The Ministries of Construction and Transportation are responsible for organising major public works projects, some of which are carried out by public corporations established by the government. Although these projects are open to competitive bidding, construction companies must be licensed, technically qualified and designated to participate in the bidding process. In the past, few foreign construction firms applied to obtain licenses for work in Japan. During 1988, six US companies, four Korean companies and one European company were granted Japanese construction licenses. There is expected to be greater foreign participation in Japan's major construction projects, including the Kansai International Airport and the Trans-Tokyo Bay Highway.

C. Europe

Most European countries have Ministries of Construction, which among other activities, sponsor and coordinate research and development; in addition, the European Community supports cooperative construction-related research programmes. As part of the removal of barriers to trade within the European market by 1992, the EEC is working to develop European-wide building standards and engineering qualifications as well as to open up bidding on public works contracts to international competition. Most European construction markets are now protected through national norms and local preference provisions. In anticipation of a more competitive construction market in the 1990s, restructuring of the construction industry is ongoing with an increased number of mergers, acquisitions and joint ventures among engineering and construction firms.

All European countries maintain export financing systems, which provide insurance and credits to overseas contractors, and many provide market information and promotion assistance and maintain a network of ties and agreements with developing countries which benefit the construction industry. The services provided by European governments to assist the construction sector tend to be more extensive than those in the United States and Japan, although the level and rate of financing vary greatly by country. In France, aid funds extended by the Treasury are generally associated with private export credits under a scheme for mixed credits established in the early 1960s. Italy's bilateral aid funds are associated with export credits if a project requires additional finance. Under the United Kingdom's Aid and Trade Provision established in 1977, funds from the UK aid budget are available in combination with export credits if a project is of commercial interest to the United Kingdom and of developmental value for the recipient. The EEC has recently begun drafting proposals to harmonize the export credit policies of the European countries, which would make it easier for European firms to collaborate in bidding on foreign projects.

The European Community protested the 1988 bilateral agreement between Japan and the United States regarding opening of the Japanese construction market fearing that European firms might be discriminated against in gaining access to Japan's public works projects. The EEC is now reviewing potential obstacles to participation by European firms in Japan's public works competition and negotiating with the Japanese government for increased access.

D.   Non-OECD Countries

Improvement in construction capacity has been a major goal of the development process and a cornerstone of industrialisation in non-OECD countries who have followed import substitution and export promotion strategies with regard to construction. Governments in these countries have enacted regulations requiring foreign construction and design engineering firms to subcontract with local companies, form joint ventures with national firms or procure local materials and supplies. The growing capabilities and technical expertise of non-OECD construction firms has helped them obtain an increasing share of work in their domestic markets and contributed to the decline in non-OECD markets for international construction. An increasing number of non-OECD contractors are now competing internationally, with firms from Korea, Taiwan, India and Brazil placing among the top international firms in the 1980s.

Korea's construction industry has had the most success in international markets, although its world market share has declined in recent years due to the downturn in the Middle East market and the loss of comparative advantage in low labour costs. The Korean government through the Ministry of Construction has a long history of involvement in the construction industry including keeping wages competitively low, sponsoring research and development, obtaining foreign technology and protecting the domestic market. Development of a design engineering sector has been encouraged under provisions of the Engineering Services Promotion Law of 1973. The Korean market is generally closed to foreign contractors and design engineers through a pre-designated bidding system and requirements for specialised skills and local registration. No foreign contractors have business licences to perform construction in Korea at this time. The Korean Government also provides financing assistance and export credit packages to assist the construction industry in competing abroad and supports counter-trade agreements with other countries. In an attempt to make this sector more internationally competitive, the government announced in 1986 that it would reduce the pool of overseas general construction firms by a third to some 30 firms and would encourage firms to explore new markets in Asia and North America. The restructuring process has included government management of contractors and tax incentives to contractors taking over insolvent companies.

V. MAJOR ISSUES

A. Barriers to Trade in Services

Trade in construction services is limited by barriers to imports of these services in both OECD and non-OECD countries. Some trade barriers, which are common to many services sectors, stem from the fact that construction requires a presence at the site where the service is purchased. It thus invokes employment, presence and financial issues which are substantially different from barriers to trade in manufacturing. Other barriers to trade, primarily related to regulations and procurement, result from the view that construction is inherently a domestic industry supported by a local labour force. In many cases, these policies have been imposed for legitimate domestic economic, political or security purposes.

There are certain barriers to trade in construction services – common to many OECD and non-OECD countries   – which are often unintentional obstacles to imports (see Table 43). In almost all countries, problems are caused to overseas construction and design engineering firms by difficulties and delays in obtaining work permits and licenses; such administrative obstacles may be due to bureaucratic inefficiencies or deliberate attempts to reduce imports. All countries have national safety and building regulations and technical standards which can also constitute intentional or unintentional barriers to construction trade, particularly if they lack transparency or are rigidly applied. Most countries restrict the level of foreign workers through visa requirements, although some allow temporary residence by skilled employees. Requirements for the requalification of professional and technical personnel can be an effective limit on the use of skilled personnel overseas and has been an especially onerous restriction on exports by design engineering firms.

Other types of trade barriers are more common in non-OECD countries (although not confined to these countries) due to their desire to enhance local construction capabilities and speed technology transfer as well as to their general financing problems. These are primarily government requirements for some form of local presence whether a joint venture, local equity or subsidiary; for local hiring of construction workers and engineering personnel; and for local procurement of materials and equipment. Tariffs or quotas may be placed on imported materials to encourage local purchases; such restrictions highlight the dual nature of the construction sector which has both goods and services aspects. Due to financial difficulties in non-OECD countries, foreign firms may encounter problems due to failure to pay for services or delays in payment, tax regimes that discriminate against foreign companies and restrictions on foreign exchange transactions.

One of the major barriers to trade in OECD markets is discrimination in government procurement to protect local markets and maintain employment. Public works constitute a large share of non-residential construction and governments tend to maintain provisions which

Table 43. **Barriers to Trade in Construction Services**

Type	Most prevalent in:
Administrative obstacles	All countries
Technical regulations	All countries
Labour/professional restrictions	All countries
Local presence or equity requirements	Non-OECD countries
Local employment requirements	Non-OECD countries
Source materials requirements	Non-OECD countries
Exchange control requirements	Non-OECD countries
Tax and payment regimes	Non-OECD countries
Public procurement limitations	OECD countries
Export subsidies	OECD countries

Source: OECD, Working Party of the Trade Committee, "Trade in Services: Examination of the Relevance of the Conceptual Framework: Construction Engineering", 29 October 1987.

favour domestic firms in obtaining such contracts. Preferences may be given outright to national construction companies or may be applied to small and medium-sized enterprises or firms from certain regions. Public entities may give a discount to national firms when comparing bid prices for government construction projects or use pre-designated bidding systems in qualifying only a short list of firms or consultants to place bids. Most OECD countries have placed some restrictions on participation by foreign firms in government-financed or government-regulated projects. The United Kingdom limits design contracts on North Sea oil projects to British firms. While the US construction market is relatively open, participation by foreign contractors may be limited by state and local government preference laws, set-asides for disadvantaged business enterprises and restrictions on foreign firms for certain public construction projects abroad. Export subsidies, which can cause distortions in international competition in construction, are considered the other major barrier to trade in construction services practiced by the OECD countries; these are discussed in the next section.

The OECD is updating and revising the Codes of Liberalization of Current Invisible Operations and Capital Movements to provide more comprehensive coverage of services activities and sharpen the effectiveness of these Codes in promoting liberalisation in services trade. These codes have already been amended to strengthen coverage in the fields of insurance, travel and tourism, audiovisual and, most recently, banking and financial services. In addition, the National Treatment provisions of the OECD Declaration on International Investment and Multinational Enterprises states that all countries should treat foreign-owned companies the same as domestically owned ones. Most exceptions to national treatment are sector specific and the majority of exceptions concern the services sector. On the basis of notifications by Member countries, there are no specific restrictions concerning construction, although a few countries have exceptions in respect of government procurement relating to the provision of international consultancy services. The Committee on International Investment and Multinational Enterprises (CIME) examination of service sector measures led to an OECD Council recommendation in March 1989 which suggested ways and means of removing or relaxing discriminatory measures. Presently the CIME is working towards a new and strengthened national treatment instrument under which Member countries will take legally binding commitments on standstill and rollback of restrictive measures.

Issues related to trade in services are included on the agenda of the Uruguay Round of the GATT negotiations. The OECD Trade Committee has developed a set of general principles relevant to trade in services (the OECD Conceptual Framework for Trade in Services) to assist Member governments in the GATT negotiations. Elements of this conceptual framework include principles and concepts such as transparency, progressive liberalization of national treatment, market access and establishment, elimination of trade distorting measures, etc. Factor movements may be considered part of trade when demonstrated to be "essential" to the supplier of a service. In regard to trade in construction services, the issue of whether this is a good or service is not totally settled. Most OECD countries would be likely to support provisions for national treatment and increased transparency in pre-qualification and bidding procedures. The OECD countries also support greater mobility of highly skilled professionals such as engineers and architects. Many developing countries would support modification of labour certification requirements which would increase the mobility of their construction workforces. Some countries have called for a special GATT Code for construction services as an Annex to a general GATT agreement on services trade. There have also been proposals for an extension of the existing GATT Agreement on Government Procurement and other relevant GATT Codes to cover construction and other services as well as goods.

The services sector, which is becoming increasingly international in nature, should realise important efficiency gains from the liberalization of trade. Significant progress in developing an agreement on liberalizing services trade was represented by the mid-term review of the Uruguay Round of the GATT in December 1988. However, some difficult issues remain to be resolved, including those relating to general concepts such as national treatment and reciprocity and their application to different services sectors. In regard to trade in construction services, the labour mobility issues pose some difficult questions for the OECD countries. Nevertheless, it is generally agreed that greater harmonization and liberalization of national policies affecting services through the OECD Codes and the GATT negotiations will enhance trade and fair competition in construction and other services.

B.   Export Subsidies

Export subsidies, which are considered an important barrier to trade in construction services, are included under the category of "trade-distorting measures or practices" in the OECD Conceptual Framework for Trade in Services. The GATT Code on Subsidies and Countervailing Duties covers export subsidies for manufactured products and defines them primarily as failure to cover the costs of export credit insurance, export credits at less than the cost of funds and financing the costs of obtaining export credits. This Code requires developed-country signatories to apply the provisions of the OECD Arrangement on Guidelines for Officially Supported Export Credits, which are pertinent to both services and manufacturing industries. Export subsidies for services such as construction have thus been debated primarily within the context of the OECD Arrangement. In general, some countries support limiting the conditions under which export subsidies are allowed, while others favour eliminating export subsidies altogether.

OECD governments provide different types of support to national firms, including those in the construction sector, in winning contracts abroad. In general, competition in the use of export aid to win foreign contracts is believed to be growing in the OECD area in the 1980s. Table 44 shows the level and content of financial flows from the DAC Member countries to non-OECD countries in 1986. About half of the bilateral aid commitments of the DAC Member

Table 44. **OECD Financial Flows to non-OECD Countries: 1986**

	Total Bilateral Aid (mil US$)	Of which Tied Aid[1] (%)	Associated Financing[2] (mil US$)	Export Credits[3] (%)
Australia	524	50	16	501
Austria	141	97	0	103
Belgium[4]	355	57	3	226
Canada	1 003	55	11	449
Denmark	485	37	127	108
Finland	179	54	27	44
France[4]	4 162	57	1 240	804
Germany	3 341	35	0	2 379
Ireland[4]	25	33	0	32
Italy	1 452	90	220	1 127
Japan	4 527	41	91	4 215
Netherlands	1 199	43	65	620
New Zealand	58	43	0	1
Norway	453	23	0	784
Sweden	734	31	252	784
Switzerland[4]	323	30	46	577
United Kingdom	1 092	78	448	3 438
United States	8 017	55	0	2 638
Total	28 070	50	2 554	18 830

1. Includes partially untied aid.
2. Includes mixed credits.
3. Includes official and private export credits.
4. Bilateral aid is net disbursements.
Source: OECD Creditor Reporting System.

countries was tied to purchases of goods and services in the donor country. Associated financing transactions including mixed credits, which combine export credits with official development aid, accounted for about 8 per cent of bilateral aid flows from the DAC Member countries. About $19 billion of government and private export credits were also extended in 1986 to assist exports to non-OECD countries.

Export credit finance systems, which can be instrumental in the success of contractors in foreign markets, vary significantly from country to country. All DAC countries provide some type of export credit insurance. About half of these governments provide export financing, while other countries have private export credit institutions; however, it is often difficult to distinguish public and private sources of export credit financing. Finance for export credit can be made available as either supplier or buyer credit; the latter – where the exporter's bank or other financial institution lends to the buyer – is more often used in the construction industry. The export credit systems of Japan, Germany, France and the United Kingdom are fairly extensive while that of the United States has been boosted in recent years. More importantly, these systems have differed in their degree of interest rate subsidies. However, this aspect of financial competition has been reduced in recent years through modifications to the OECD Arrangement as well as by the decline in interest rates after 1982.

A smaller number of governments extend mixed credits, which act to subsidise industrial exports through the mixture of aid and export credits. The decrease in the provision of export credits with interest rate subsidies has been accompanied by an increase in the use of mixed credits in the 1980s. France, where the use of mixed credits originated, has in most years accounted for about half of the total amount of associated financing among the DAC countries; it is estimated that about 10 per cent of all official credit transactions in France are financed through mixed credit. Mixed credits generally account for a higher than average share of aid flows in Italy, Japan, Denmark, Sweden, the Netherlands and the United Kingdom. Countries such as the United Kingdom and the United States use mixed credits mainly for matching purposes, i.e., in support of national exporters competing against foreign offers involving official financial support.

The OECD Arrangement on Guidelines for Officially Supported Export Credits, which came into being in April 1978, is intended to prevent an export credit race in which countries compete on the basis of financing terms rather than on the quality and price of their goods and services. This Arrangement sets limits on the terms and conditions of export credits including minimun interest rates, minimum down payments and maximum payback periods; participants are not supposed to subsidise export credits below the established levels. The Arrangement also sets limits on mixed credits including the minimum grant element in a tied aid package. In 1987, the Arrangement participants accepted a new and much more restrictive agreement on the use of export credits. Mixed credits are now only permitted if the grant element is equal to at least 35 per cent of the total package, and the rules for calculating the grant element have been changed to reflect variations in national interest rates; this is intended to prevent lower interest rate countries from having an advantage over countries with higher interest rates.

Some countries, including the United States, Canada and some of the smaller European countries, have supported the elimination of the subsidy element of export credits. Subsidised export financing is believed to frustrate the economic role of the cost of credit and lead to an inefficient use of resources as well as unfair trade competition. Other countries believe the Arrangement provides for the controlled use of export subsidies and does not need to be further altered. There is also continuing debate regarding the use of associated financing in aid flows and how it may distort export credits. Some countries want the grant element to be further increased or mixed credits eliminated altogether, while others believe that mixed credits are a positive part of a donor country's aid policy. Given the market situation in construction and national views on the use of mixed credits, it is probable that there will continue to be competition based on financing terms in this industry. OECD countries need to continue to work together through the Arrangement to regulate the use of export subsidies and increase compliance with the Arrangement. In the long run, commercially realistic terms for export credits will lead to better use of scarce resources, enhanced development aid and fairer competition in industries such as construction.

C. Industrial Policies for Services

General debate over industrial policies has generally concerned manufacturing rather than services industries. Few governments have had active policies toward the services side of their economies. As trade in services is liberalised, competitive pressures on services sectors such as construction will increase. There is growing recognition of the links between the competitiveness of manufacturing and services sectors and the need for governments to consider interrelated policy approaches. Industrial policymakers may want to give more attention to performance in services sectors and to factors such as services data, research, productivity, restructuring and global strategies. They may also wish to consider new institutional mechanisms for coordinating policies (e.g., regulatory, technology and trade) for services industries and integrating these with manufacturing policies and programmes.

Increased trade in services such as design engineering and construction will expand markets for manufactured goods from the OECD countries. The construction industry is believed to generate the highest level of associated goods exports of any services sector. Merchandise sales generally follow from exports of construction services partly because design engineers tend to specify equipment and materials with which they are familiar; further exports of equipment may stem from demand for spare and replacement parts. A US Government survey in the early l980s showed that 33 out of 38 American design and construction firms specified US equipment for their projects; other surveys have found that an average 80 per cent of the equipment used in foreign construction projects may be imported from the home country of the contractor. Conversely, the competitiveness of manufactured exports can directly affect the construction sector. The technical excellence and reliability of the engineering equipment and machine tools industries in Germany and Japan have helped their construction firms in winning overseas contracts.

OECD governments have recognised the need to improve data collection and analysis of services activities, particularly trade in services. Better statistics will increase the understanding of the linkages between services and manufacturing and contribute to evaluating future prospects for construction and other services sectors and developing effective negotiating strategies in the GATT. At present, there are a number of discrepancies in the way different countries report receipts from foreign construction and engineering activities, reflecting mainly differences in statistical categories and in practices with regard to distinguishing investment income from services income. Under the auspices of the OECD Trade Committee, work is being carried out to collect and improve statistics on trade in services, including construction statistics. As part of this work, the OECD is also contributing to broader international work on definitions and classifications for services, including the revision of the International Standard Industrial Classification (ISIC) to broaden its services coverage.

Some services sectors including construction have a low level of investment in research and development relative to turnover. This may be one reason why productivity levels in such services have lagged behind those in manufacturing and agriculture. In the international construction industry, it appears that research is concentrated in a few large multinationals in a small number of OECD countries. At the national level, construction research is generally fragmented among small firms. While most construction technology is available through licensing, innovation in construction methods and proprietary rights for new technologies can add to competitiveness through reducing costs and improving productivity. As services become more important to the balance of trade in OECD countries, governments may want to review the level of investment in research and the organisation of technology efforts in construction and other services sectors.

OECD governments may also wish to encourage construction companies, most of which are domestically-oriented, to approach markets in global rather than national terms and to increase their export orientation. However, the structure of the construction industry in many OECD countries is not conducive to successful international competition. As trade pressures increase, construction firms may need to consolidate activities, sell unprofitable operations and acquire firms to complement existing abilities. National and international mergers and acquisitions are already on the upswing in the OECD construction sector as firms prepare for European market integration in l992 and attempt to increase their presence in the large US and Japanese construction markets. There may also be a need for diversification of construction companies to new functional or geographic areas as a shield against cyclical and regional variations in demand for construction services.

Construction firms working in overseas markets will need to reappraise their sources of competitive strength and their global strategies. Although demand may improve in the long-run due to removal of trade barriers, revival of Middle East activity, new Soviet approaches to private sector involvement and/or improvement in the debt situation of the developing countries, competition in international construction will remain intense. In particular, competition in OECD construction markets is expected to grow. The need for OECD construction firms to cut costs, package construction services, increase technology content and seek out global bidding partners will intensify. OECD industrial policymakers may wish to consider these needs and the adequacy of government policy approaches for services sectors.

REFERENCES

Commission of the European Communities (1988), "Panorama of EC Industry: 1989", Luxembourg.

Engineering News Record, various issues.

Euro-Construct (1989), "Proceedings of Conference on European Construction: 1988-1992", United Kingdom, National Economic Development Office.

Japanese Research Institute of Construction and Economy (1988), "Structure and Characteristics of the Construction Industry in Japan", October.

OECD, (1987, 1988), *Development Co-Operation Reports,* Development Assistance Committee.

OECD (1987), *The Export Credit Financing Systems in OECD Member Countries.*

OECD (1988), "Mastering Technology: Engineering Services Firms in Developing Countries", Development Centre.

Suter, H. (1988), "L'industrie du bâtiment en mutation", *Vie économique,* February.

US Department of Commerce (1989), *A Competitive Assessment of the U.S. International Construction Industry,* Washington, DC.

US Office of Technology Assessment (1987), *International Competition in Services,* Washington DC, July.

THE SEMICONDUCTOR INDUSTRY

I. SUMMARY

The product and geographic profile of the semiconductor industry in the 1980s is becoming more diversified. The product structure of the industry is evolving towards a wider range of custom devices for electronics systems. Demand has shifted from the United States and Europe towards Japan and other Asian countries, which now account for 51 per cent of world semiconductor consumption. Japan has surpassed the United States in world market share of merchant semiconductor production, while output of different types of semiconductors is being increasingly dispersed among countries.

These trends have been accompanied by growing semiconductor trade frictions centering on memory circuits (primarily DRAMs) which accounted for 22 per cent of semiconductor output in 1988. DRAMs are often considered the "technology driver" of the semiconductor industry. Japanese firms now dominate DRAM production having greatly increased market share through investment in equipment and research, an emphasis on mass production techniques, exchange rate advantages and the ability to produce at lower costs. US companies, which maintain a competitive advantage in design and product technology, dominate the market for other types of semiconductors such as microprocessors and custom devices. European firms and newer producers in other countries are developing strengths in several areas of semiconductor production through concerted R&D programmes.

The following are the major policy issues identified:

a) *Technology and Pricing:* Competition in semiconductors is partially dependent on the ability of producers to move down technology- and learning-based cost curves. The pricing strategies of semiconductor firms may be based on these learning economies or on more aggressive attempts to increase market share. Such pricing ambiguities have raised questions about the definition of dumping in international trade.

b) *New Types of Trade Measures:* New types of measures called grey-area measures are being used as trade policy instruments for semiconductors and other products. Some have argued that such measures may incur higher costs than benefits and it may be useful to clarify them within the GATT context.

c) *Industrial Policies for High-Technology Industries:* Many countries view an indigenous semiconductor industry as essential to economic growth and national security. While some countries need to maintain a semiconductor production base which includes the capability to produce memories for defence and economic reasons, this need may be declining in other countries due to the internationalisation of production and marketing and changing product demand. Governments should review the configuration of their semiconductor industries and the best combination of industrial and trade policy instruments for maintaining competitiveness.

II. INDUSTRY BACKGROUND

A. Product Structure

The semiconductor industry produces electronic components based on materials, primarily silicon, which can act alternately as conductors allowing electrical current to flow or as insulators stopping this flow. These components form the basis of the electronics industry. There are three major categories of semiconductors: *i)* discrete or individual devices; *ii)* integrated circuits which have many devices fabricated onto a single chip; and *iii)* optoelectronic devices which respond to or emit light (see Table 45). Discrete devices account for a declining share of total semiconductor sales. Integrated circuits account for the largest and fastest-growing share of semiconductor sales. Optoelectronic devices are relatively new but are gradually increasing their share of total production.

Integrated circuits are divided into different types: *i)* memories which store information; *ii)* custom circuits which are designed for individual applications; *iii)* linear circuits which process analog or continuous signals; *iv)* logic circuits which process instructions and data according to rules of logic; and *v)* microprocessors which are complex logic chips that often include some memory.

Table 45. **Product Structure of World Semiconductor Market: 1988**

	World Sales[1] (mil US$)	Share (%)
Discrete devices	9 000	15
Integrated circuits	50 500	81
Memories	14 000	22
Linear	10 500	17
Custom	9 500	15
Microprocessors	6 800	11
Logic	6 700	11
Special Purpose	3 000	5
Optoelectronic devices	2 500	4
Total	62 000	100

1. Merchant and captive semiconductor sales in current US dollars.
Source: OECD estimates.

Memory devices accounted for 22 per cent of semiconductor sales in 1988 and an estimated 29 per cent in 1989 and are the subject of intense trade competition. Random access memories (RAMs), which temporarily store data or instructions, include the large-capacity Dynamic RAMs (DRAMs) and the higher speed Static RAMs (SRAMS). Each generation of DRAMs, which account for 12 per cent or more of the world semiconductor market, holds four times as much information as the generation before. There has been a rapid progression from the 1K (one thousand bit or one kilobit) DRAM in 1970 to the 64K DRAM in 1979, the 256K DRAM in 1985, and the 4M (four-megabit) DRAM in 1989. There are goals for the 16M DRAM by 1991 and the 64M DRAM by the mid-1990s. Other popular memory devices are Read Only Memories (ROMs), which store data more permanently and include Erasable Programmable ROMs (EPROMs) and Electrically Erasable Programmable ROMs (EEPROMs).

Custom devices, which account for about 15 per cent of semiconductor sales, are the fastest growing type of integrated circuit, especially application specific integrated circuits (ASICs) which are made for individual customers or uses. It is forecast that ASICs will rise to 25 per cent of the world semiconductor market by the mid-1990s.

The sale of microprocessors has grown to account for about 11 per cent of world semiconductor sales. Higher sales volumes reflect continued strong demand for microprocessors from the makers of personal computers, work stations and computer-aided design systems. Demand is expected to increase for reduced instruction set computing (RISC) chips, a newer high-speed microprocessor used in desktop work stations. More mature integrated circuit products, such as linear circuits and standard logic devices, have had relatively lower demand growth in recent years although they still account for 28 per cent of total semiconductor production.

B. Industry Structure

Global production of semiconductors is highly concentrated with the top ten firms producing 50 per cent of output. In 1987, ten Japanese, seven American and three European firms accounted for over 70 per cent of worldwide semiconductor production. The Korean firm Samsung had the strongest growth in 1988 to give it over 1 per cent of the world market (see q Table 46). This production consists of merchant production for the external market and captive production for internal company production of electronic systems.

The semiconductor industry in the United States is composed of diversely structured producers. IBM is the largest US firm but its semiconductor output is mostly for internal use. Approximately 35 per cent of US output is captive production. Specifically, about 20 per cent of US production is by captive divisions of large integrated companies, such as IBM; 22 per cent is by diversified electronics and aerospace firms with both merchant and captive production but mostly captive; 24 per cent is by diversified electronics firms with mostly merchant sales, such as Motorola and Texas Instruments; 20 per cent is by merchant semiconductor firms which produce and sell a broad range of semiconductor products, such as Intel and National Semiconductor; and 14 per cent is by small merchant companies with speciality or niche products.

The Japanese and European semiconductor industries consist mostly of large electronics firms which engage primarily in merchant sales with smaller captive production. The ten largest Japanese firms, led by NEC, Toshiba and Hitachi, are vertically integrated electronics compa-

136

Table 46. **Principal Semiconductor Manufacturers: 1988**

	Company Headquarters	Estimated Production (Mil US$)	Total World Market Share (%)
NEC	Japan	4 500	7.3
IBM	US	4 400	7.1
Toshiba	Japan	4 300	6.9
Hitachi	Japan	3 600	5.8
Motorola	US	3 000	4.8
Texas Instruments	US	2 700	4.4
Fujitsu	Japan	2 400	3.9
Intel	US	2 350	3.8
Mitsubishi	Japan	2 300	3.7
Matsushita	Japan	1 900	3.1
Philips-Signetics	Netherlands	1 800	2.9
National Semiconductor	US	1 700	2.7
Advanced Micro Devices	US	1 100	1.8
Sanyo	Japan	1 090	1.8
SGS-Thomson	Italy/France	1 080	1.8
Sharp	Japan	1 040	1.7
OKI	Japan	950	1.5
Sony	Japan	920	1.5
Samsung	Korea	900	1.5
AT&T	US	860	1.4
Siemens	Germany	780	1.3
Total	21 firms	43 670	70.0

Source: Dataquest.

nies for which semiconductors account for less than 25 per cent of total sales. The Japanese industry is highly concentrated with the five largest firms accounting for about 60 per cent of semiconductor production and more than 75 per cent of integrated circuit production. Philips, Siemens, SGS-Thomson and Telefunken account for over 80 per cent of production by European-based firms. Europe also has several smaller firms, such as INMOS and Plessey in the United Kingdom, which are important in niche markets. Semiconductor production in the NIEs is led by the three large Korean groups Samsung, Hyundai and Goldstar.

C. Demand Trends

Semiconductor demand is related to electronics systems demand, which is both fast-growing and volatile. Computers account for about 40 per cent of world semiconductor consumption. The second major end use, accounting for about 20 per cent of consumption, is a variety of consumer goods such as radios, televisions and stereos. Other uses are telecommunications equipment (about 15 per cent), industrial electronics equipment (12 per cent), military uses (8 per cent) and transportation equipment (5 percent). National semiconductor consumption patterns differ according to the structure of the electronics industry. Military uses account for less than 10 per cent of the semiconductor market in the United States and for very little in Japan; consumer electronics account for 34 per cent of consumption in Japan and about 6 per

Table 47. **Geographic Structure of World Semiconductor Market**[1]

Percentages

	1960	1970	1982	1988	1990
United States	75	53	49	31	30
Japan	10	22	26	39	40
Europe	12	22	20	18	17
Others	3	3	5	12	13
Total	100	100	100	100	100

1. Share of world consumption in current US dollars.
Source: Electronics, various issues.

cent in the United States. In Europe, the two major categories of demand are consumer electronics and telecommunications systems.

The growth rate of semiconductor demand since the beginning of commercial production in the 1950s has been rapid. But like demand for electronic systems and other capital goods, semiconductor demand is highly cyclical, a trait which is exacerbated by the introduction of new semiconductor products and technologies. From the 1950s to the early 1980s, worldwide semiconductor demand rose by an average 17 per cent per year. In 1984, semiconductor demand surged by over 40 per cent due to increasing sales of personal computers, leading to higher prices and increased investment in new capacity. However, demand fell sharply in 1985 causing severe oversupply problems in 1985 and 1986. In 1987, a recovery in demand led to a 24 per cent increase in semiconductor sales followed by 32 per cent growth in 1988.

The OECD countries account for about 90 per cent of semiconductor consumption, but non-OECD countries such as Korea, Taiwan, Singapore and Hong Kong are rapidly increasing their share of world demand (see Table 47). Overall, semiconductor consumption in non-OECD countries is rising more rapidly than in the OECD countries. The Japanese market outgrew both the United States and European markets to become the largest consumer of semiconductor products in 1986. The marked increase in the Japanese consumption share is due to both the growth in electronics production and the shift in exchange rates. The European countries, where Germany is the largest electronics market, has evidenced a declining share of world semiconductor demand as has the United States. These trends are expected to continue to 1990 with Japan and the Asian NIEs, including Korea, Taiwan, Singapore, Hong Kong, the Philippines and Thailand, experiencing the most dramatic demand growth. Some forecasts indicate that the Asian NIEs, who are increasingly using semiconductors in domestic production of consumer electronics products and other electronics systems, may surpass Europe in semiconductor consumption by 1992.

D. Production Trends

In 1988, total world semiconductor production (both captive and merchant sales) was estimated at $62 billion. Merchant sales of semiconductors were estimated at about $50 billion. Japanese and US companies dominate world semiconductor production accounting for almost

Table 48.   **Trends in World Semiconductor Sales**[1]

	1978		1988	
	Sales (mil. US$)	Share (%)	Sales (mil. US$)	Share (%)
United States	10 230	62	18 500	37
Japan	4 620	28	25 000	50
Europe	1 650	10	5 000	10
Other	0	0	1 500	3
Total world	16 500	100	50 000	100

1. Merchant semiconductor sales in current US dollars based on nationality of firm headquarters.
Source: Dataquest.

90 per cent of global output. Japanese firms have surpassed US companies in world market share and accounted for about half of world merchant semiconductor sales in dollar terms in 1988 (see Table 48). Japanese and US firms have more equal world market shares when captive production is included. European firms and those of the Asian NIEs are estimated to have a total of over $6 billion in merchant semiconductor sales in 1988.

The most significant development in global semiconductor production has been the increase in Japanese output from 28 per cent of world production in the late 1970s to 50 per cent in 1988. The US industry has been rapidly losing market share to the Japanese, particularly in the mid-1980s. Between 1978 and 1988, US market share (excluding captive sales) of global semiconductor production fell from 62 per cent to 37 per cent. The loss in US market share partly reflects changes in exchange rates and the slower growth of North American and European markets compared to the rapid growth in the Japanese market which is supplied primarily by Japanese firms. European firms have failed to gain as strong a position as the United States or Japan, but have maintained about a 10 per cent market share over the last decade. The market share of non-OECD companies, principally firms from the Asian NIEs, has increased to 3 per cent since 1978.

These aggregate production figures, however, disguise divergences in shares in individual semiconductor product markets (see Table 49). Japan dominates the world market for DRAMs. After the sharp price drop of 1985-86, Japanese firms emerged with most of the DRAM market while US producers dropped from market dominance to a minor role. Japanese producers now account for over 80 per cent of world production of the higher capacity 256K and one-megabit DRAMs. However, US firms such as IBM (which is a captive producer), Texas Instruments, Micron Technology and Motorola maintain DRAM production and other US firms are considering reentering the memories market. US firms dominate the market for specialised memory chips such as EEPROMS. European firms have also focused on more specialised memories. Newer manufacturers from the NIEs are concentrating their efforts on the production of higher-volume semiconductor memories.

US firms have their strongest showing in the production of microprocessors, where they account for about 70 per cent of world output. Firms such as Intel and Motorola dominate this market, where product design and customer relations are more important than yields and prices. Intel has proprietorship of the most widely-used 32-bit microprocessor, which is produced by

Table 49. **Semiconductor Market Shares by Selected Product: 1988**[1]

Percentages

	US	Japan	Europe	NICs	Total
DRAMs	15	72	5	8	100
Other memory circuits	48	39	10	3	100
Microprocessors	70	18	9	3	100
Custom circuits	52	35	12	1	100

1. Estimated share of merchant sales in current US dollars based on nationality of firm headquarters.
Source: OECD estimates.

several US semiconductor firms, and American companies are the major producers of the newer RISC microprocessors. Most microprocessors from Japanese, European and NIE firms are produced under American second-source licensing agreements. In an attempt to create a new market, the Japanese firms Hitachi, Fujitsu and Mitsubishi have formed the Global Microprocessor Group to develop and produce 32-bit microprocessors and new designs based on an open architecture TRON.

Future trade competition is expected to be intense in custom chips, which have been mostly produced by US firms. Japan is turning its attention to this area and in 1988 came to rival the United States in the production of the fast-growing, semi-custom ASIC chips. US firms still account for about 55 per cent of output of custom semiconductors but may be losing market share. In the past, Japanese producers concentrated on RAM technology, American producers on microprocessor and custom chip technology, and European producers on logic circuits. These product associations are changing as countries other than the United States intensify their research on more specialised semiconductor products.

E. Trade and Foreign Investment Trends

Statistics on semiconductor trade balances present a confusing picture due to the high degree of offshore manufacturing and associated imports and exports. Most trade is in commodity memories and in semiconductor parts for reassembly. Trade has accounted for relatively minor shares of direct sales of products other than DRAMs and other memories. As shown in Table 50, most OECD countries have deficits in semiconductor trade except for Japan which has a surplus: Japan also has the lowest level of import penetration. In the case of both the United States and Japan, about half of total imports and exports are generated by offshore manufacturing: parts of semiconductors are exported to non-OECD or other OECD countries where they are assembled and reexported often back to the source country. The European trade data also includes a substantial share of intrafirm trade, including imports and reexports of semiconductor parts by foreign manufacturers.

A more accurate picture of market trends is given in Table 51, which shows the share held by US, Japanese and European firms in their respective regional markets. In 1988, Japanese firms accounted for about 18 per cent of US merchant sales of semiconductors with memories constituting the chief Japanese semiconductor product sold in the United States. US trade in semiconductors has been in deficit since 1982 which marked the increase in imports of Japanese

Table 50.   **OECD Semiconductor Trade: 1988**

	Trade balance (mil. US$)	Import penetration[1] (%)	Export shares[2] (%)
United States	−1 140	32	28
Japan	4 800	11	34
United Kingdom[3]	−375	83	77
Germany[3]	−94	82	80
France[3]	−25	70	70
Italy[3]	−290	87	82
Canada	−330	97	75
Australia	−30	83	19

1. Imports as a share of domestic consumption.
2. Exports as a share of production.
3. Includes intra-EEC trade.
Source: Based on national sources.

memory circuits. European firms account for another 2 per cent of the US market; US purchases of memories from Korean firms have increased in the past two years to now account for about 2 per cent of consumption.

US firms have historically accounted for about 10 per cent of the Japanese market. Most US sales in Japan are of non-memory products. The Asian countries have increased their exports of high-capacity DRAMs to Japan owing to shortages during 1988 and accounted for about 0.1 per cent of the market, while European firms also accounted for about 0.1 per cent of Japan's semiconductor sales. In 1989, European and Asian companies' combined share of Japan's market rose to 0.8 per cent. Foreign firms gained a slightly larger share of Japan's semiconductor market in 1990, although the exact figure is subject to dispute.

In 1988, the 12 EC countries imported or purchased from foreign firms about 50 per cent of the semiconductors they consumed. Japanese producers increased their share to 14 per cent of the West European market, while the share of US firms declined to about 36 per cent. The

Table 51.   **Semiconductor Market Shares by Region: 1988**

Percentages

Held by:	Market		
	United States	Japan	Europe
US firms	80.0	10.0	36.0
Japanese firms	18.0	89.8	14.0
European firms	2.0	0.1	49.0
Other	2.0	0.1	1.0
Total	100.0	100.0	100.0

Source: OECD estimates.

Table 52. **Semiconductor Market Shares by Nationality and Location of Production: 1988**

Percentages

	Production Share by Firm Headquarters		Production Share by Location	
	1978	1988	1978	1988
United States	62	37	60	34
Japan	28	50	24	40
Europe	10	10	9	12
Other	0	3	7	14
Total	100	100	100	100

Source: OECD and Dataquest.

Japanese share in some segments of the European market such as high-density DRAMs is relatively high, while US firms maintain a large share of the microprocessor market. In the European market, Philips held the number one place in 1988 followed by SGS-Thomson, Texas Instruments, Motorola and Siemens. Other manufacturers, mainly Korean, accounted for 1 per cent of sales. The European countries exported about $2 billion of semiconductor products in 1988 mostly to the United States and Japan, but still had an overall trade deficit with these countries.

The extent of foreign investment in semiconductor manufacturing is indicated in the differences in market share by nationality of firm and by the location of production (see Table 52). The United States and Japan together have based about 13 per cent of their production in European and other countries. Japanese manufacturing facilities in the United States, and to a lesser extent, US manufacturing facilities in Japan, account for a share of this production. Overall, other countries have increased their share of output while the United States has become less important as a locale for semiconductor production. Table 53 gives a more detailed account of semiconductor production based on the location of output.

US firms have long maintained operations for assembly of semiconductor parts in lower-wage countries such as Malaysia, Singapore, the Philippines, Korea and Mexico. At one time, almost 90 per cent of the semiconductors sold abroad by US firms were assembled at offshore locations; this percentage has declined in the 1980s with the construction of domestic automated assembly facilities. US companies also operate many higher technology fabrication facilities in European regions such as Ireland and Scotland. The European semiconductor firms have invested relatively less in foreign facilities, although Philips and other companies are now moving some activities to lower-cost Asian and Latin American locations.

Japanese companies retain most assembly operations in Japan and are investing in highly automated facilities. Japanese firms have also invested in Asia and in a few assembly and testing operations in Europe to aid market penetration. Recently, Japanese semiconductor companies have established and acquired more higher value-added fabrication facilities in Europe, the United States and other locations. In 1988, Japan had 152 electronic component production facilities overseas: over three-fourths of these in the Asian NIEs primarily Korea and Taiwan, 12 facilities in Europe and 20 in the United States. Japanese firms are increasing foreign investment in the semiconductor industry due largely to exchange rate considerations and the need to circumvent trade barriers.

Table 53. **Semiconductor Sales by Location of Production**[1]

	1978		1988	
	Value (mil. US$)	Share (%)	Value (mil. US$)	Share (%)
United States	9 900	60	17 000	34
Japan	3 100	24	20 000	40
Europe	1 500	9	6 000	12
Germany			1 600	
France			1 500	
United Kingdom			1 260	
Italy			350	
Austria			45	
Belgium			10	
Denmark			6	
Finland			30	
Ireland			250	
Netherlands			600	
Norway			10	
Portugal			120	
Spain			30	
Sweden			200	
Switzerland			100	
Canada			210	
Australia			20	
Total OECD	15 000	93	43 000	86
Non-OECD	1 200	7	7 000	14
Korea			3 100	
Singapore			1 300	
Philippines			1 200	
Thailand			580	
Taiwan			530	
Hong Kong			180	
Other			110	
Total world	16 500	100	50 000	100

1. Merchant semiconductor sales in current US dollars based on location of production.
Source: OECD and *1988 Yearbook of Electronics Data*, Benn Electronics Publications, United Kingdom, 1987.

III. MAJOR COMPETITIVE FACTORS

A. Technology

Technology is the main basis of competition in the semiconductor industry. Ten years ago, US firms led the world in virtually every aspect of semiconductor technology. However, Japanese firms have achieved parity if not superiority in process technology and materials and equipment technology for semiconductor production. European and other firms remain largely dependent on technology licensed from American and Japanese companies, although their recent research efforts should give them strengths in specialised areas of semiconductor production.

Japanese firms gained their leading position in the semiconductor market partly through developing techniques for the mass production of high-quality memory devices. They were the first to realise that the market for DRAMs was growing rapidly enough to support high-volume production facilities. Through attention to process technology and management techniques, Japanese firms obtained higher yields and lower unit costs in DRAM production while providing superior performance and reliability. DRAMs, which require the highest density of devices on a chip and yields per wafer, were especially suited to Japanese state-of-the-art manufacturing methods. Factors other than technology also contributed to Japan's increase in world semiconductor market share, including supportive government policies, advantages in capital costs and pricing advantages and strategies. However, the Japanese are vulnerable to newer producers (such as the Asian NIEs) who may undercut them in price.

American companies are strong in product technology, particularly semiconductor design and software. Because Japanese firms have taken over the market in memory devices, US firms are presently most competitive in semiconductors that depend on functional design and relationships with customers, such as microprocessors and custom chips. US firms set the standard in small, flexible manufacturing facilities that can produce many different types of chips on a single production line. The growing significance of chip design for electronics systems and the increasing demand for customised chips and microdevices should benefit US producers. Japanese firms are now developing their design skills to complement their abilities at volume production.

The key to competitiveness in future semiconductor markets rests in current research and development activities. Japanese firms are investing in the development of a new generation of flexible factories and more customised product technology. Research and development in the United States is focused on traditional strengths in product design, but also on improving manufacturing techniques, developing more efficient robotised production lines and reaching Japanese quality standards. In Europe, several firms are investing in advanced computer-aided design techniques to compete in specialised markets such as ASICs. Other countries in Europe

Table 54. **Research and Development Expenditures by US and Japanese Semiconductor Firms**
Million US$

	Japanese Companies		US Companies	
	R&D Spending	% of Sales	R&D Spending	% of Sales
1978	376	15	384	8
1979	428	15	470	7
1980	484	13	625	7
1981	621	15	776	10
1982	725	16	875	11
1983	942	14	944	10
1984	1 078	11	1 414	10
1985	1 314	15	1 598	15
1986	1 760	15	1 582	14
1987	1 960	14	2 100	15

Source: OECD and Dataquest.

and Asia are considering entry into lower volume industry-specific or custom production, but the rapid pace of technological advance may remain a significant barrier to entry to the industry.

The Japanese market success is partially due to its high research and development expenditures. The semiconductor industry has one of the highest R&D intensities (ratio of R&D expenditures to sales) of any manufacturing industry. Japanese firms maintained R&D spending at a steady 12 to 15 per cent of sales throughout the past decade, while American firms let spending slip to 7 to 8 per cent of sales in the late 1970s and early 1980s (see Table 54). More recently, US research intensity has increased to 14 to 15 per cent of sales.

B. Investment

The financial resources of firms and their adaptability to investment cycles is another competitive factor in the semiconductor industry. The semiconductor market is characterised by a four-year business cycle called the silicon cycle seen in the boom years of 1980, 1984 and 1988. This, together with the short lifespan of products, creates fluctuating but massive investment requirements. Manufacturers tend to embark on capacity expansion in peak years which causes overproduction and saturated markets in lean years. This trend is being repeated in the current investment cycle in response to chip shortages, particularly of DRAMs. MITI reported that investment in plant and equipment by 11 major semiconductor manufacturers increased 40 per cent in fiscal 1988 over the previous year; the Department of Commerce reported that capital spending in the US semiconductor industry is also on the rise.

Most data show that Japanese companies invest a larger fraction of their sales income on plant and equipment than other firms (see Table 55). Some allege that large Japanese investments in semiconductor facilities are intended to increase production capacity and drive down prices. Japanese firms maintain these investments are aimed at making generation changes from lower density to higher density RAMs. New fabrication facilities for mass-produced memory

Table 55. **US and Japanese Semiconductor Investment**

Million US$

	Japanese Companies		US Companies	
	Capital spending	% of Sales	Capital spending	% of Sales
1978	453	18	650	14
1979	656	22	887	13
1980	956	25	1 300	15
1981	1 047	25	1 424	18
1982	1 301	28	1 188	15
1983	2 234	34	1 323	14
1984	3 508	36	3 010	22
1985	2 961	34	1 789	17
1986	2 586	22	1 400	13
1987	2 800	20	1 700	13

Source: OECD and Dataquest.

chips now cost about $200 million, will increase to $300 million by l990s and may eventually cost $1 billion as each new generation of products requires more sophisticated and expensive equipment. Much of Japanese investment, which incorporates clean rooms, vibration isolation and automation, is long-term and cumulative over successive chip generations. In the past, the European industry has been seriously undercapitalised compared to its US and Japanese competitors.

A competitive industry structure is important in view of the massive investment requirements of semiconductor producers. Large integrated firms, like those in Japan and Europe, can provide the resources and organisational skills needed to develop and market semiconductor innovations. Semiconductor divisions of integrated companies may be cross-subsidised by parents or affiliates, have an outlet for production in all phases of the business cycle and can link chip development more closely with the design of end products. The US industry is based in part on smaller firms with a more single product orientation. These firms may find it difficult to obtain investment funds, to shield themselves from market swings or to keep in tune with demand trends. However, many believe that smaller entrepreneurial firms are the driving force in the American semiconductor industry. They are innovative and adaptive and the venture capital system counteracts high capital costs by efficiently targeting funds. Complexity may be increasingly embedded in the chip allowing small companies to benefit while large centralised organisations lose relative efficiency.

C. Costs and Prices

Semiconductor prices, particularly of mass-produced commodity chips, are a contentious trade issue. Japan's competitors charge that Japanese firms have allegedly priced some of their products, expecially commodity memory circuits such as DRAMs and EPROMS, below the average cost of making them or below their prices in home or third markets. However, semiconductor pricing is complex and may be partially dependent on technological learning curves. Semiconductor prices reflect learning economies stemming from cumulative production

Table 56. **Evolution of Production Costs: 64 K DRAMS**[1]

	Capital		Labour		Material		Total	
	US	Japan	US	Japan	US	Japan	US	Japan
1980	3.02	7.85	5.38	6.53	4.97	8.72	13.37	23.09
1981	3.49	6.52	5.70	6.58	5.73	8.39	14.92	21.49
1982	1.62	1.97	2.82	2.22	2.49	2.51	6.93	6.69
1983	0.39	0.56	0.85	0.78	0.65	0.71	1.90	2.05
1984	0.30	0.41	0.64	0.61	0.46	0.49	1.39	1.50

1. Yielded cost per wafer in US dollars.
Source: Finan, W.F., and Amundsen, C.B. (1986), "Modeling US-Japan Competition in Semiconductors", *Journal of Policy Modeling*, 8:3.

experience, economies of scale based on volume production increases as well as the pricing policies of firms seeking to gain market share.

The semiconductor industry is somewhat unique in the rapid decline in unit costs achieved with cumulative production. This is because manufacturing experience leads to higher yields in the number of good chips per silicon wafer. Improvements in yield can continue for 18 months after introduction of a new generation of memory chips. Other determinants of cost per chip, such as equipment use rates, also improve with learning. These learning advantages can extend from one generation of chips to the next resulting in better starting yields, faster improvement rates and higher final yields.

According to one study of Japanese and US semiconductor costs, Japanese production costs for memory chips may fall more rapidly from a higher level than US costs (see Table 56). For 64K DRAMS, Japan-based manufacturers started production at a capital, labour and material cost disadvantage but drew even in the final stages of production due to higher yields and equipment use rates. Other studies have shown that Japanese learning rates may be more rapid than those of other countries due to the supply of electronics engineers, more attention to process technology and investment in automation. These studies point out the difficulty in comparing price-cost relationships across semiconductor producers at any given time for particular products.

In part, the rapid decline in prices for commodity chips reflects the cost reductions linked to manufacturing experience. Because chips in each generation are near-perfect substitutes for one another, the market for a lower capacity chip erodes very rapidly when a superior successor arrives. In general, the initial cost decline is sharper than the market price decline, giving early market entrants large price-cost margins. Many firms also engage in learning-curve pricing based on projections of sales and costs over the life-cycle of the product. Japanese firms appear to follow a more aggressive pricing strategy and a longer time horizon than other firms in profiting from learning curve advantages to gain market share.

D. Exchange Rates

Exchange rates can be an important competitive factor, particularly in the more highly traded commodity semiconductors. Marked currency appreciation can put firms at a trade disadvantage, while currency depreciation can lead to a competitive edge in both domestic and foreign markets. However, relative competitiveness depends on how firms adapt to overcome price disadvantages or develop strategies to take advantage of new market opportunities. In the past, Japanese firms have perhaps been most successful in squeezing profit margins and adjusting costs and prices to maintain market share. There is also the question of the structural effects on trade patterns and competitiveness of long-term over- or under-valuation of currency.

The exchange rate structure of the early 1980s was characterised by a strong US dollar and a weak Japanese yen. The twenty per cent rise between 1980 and 1982 in the real value of dollar, which remained high for two or three years thereafter, led to an increase in relative costs for US semiconductor producers. This occurred during a period of low world semiconductor demand, where any US price increases meant market share losses. At this time, Japanese semiconductor producers made inroads in the US market on the basis of a long undervalued yen.

In late 1985, the US dollar started its fall relative to the yen, which has since appreciated more than 80 per cent against the dollar. Japanese semiconductor producers had to either increase world market prices, cut costs severely or price below cost which would trigger antidumping complaints. Japan also had to maintain price competitiveness relative to producers in the Asian NIEs whose currencies are linked to the dollar. Japanese producers decreased their export prices in yen by more than 25 per cent. It was in late 1985, early 1986, that both the United States and the European Community initiated antidumping investigations on imports of DRAMs and EPROMs from Japan based on allegations that Japan was pricing below cost.

IV. INDUSTRIAL AND TRADE POLICIES

A. United States

The most significant factor in the early development of the US semiconductor industry was the technology pull influence of government policies. The Federal Government stimulated development of the semiconductor and computer industries during the 1950s and early 1960s through financing research and purchasing products. Military and aerospace programmes set the directions for research and development, subsidised capacity expansion to reach production levels for defence needs, encouraged the standardisation of production and guaranteed markets for some products. Military-related demand accounted for more than half of US domestic semiconductor production in the 1950s; this proportion has decreased to less than a tenth with the growth of civilian demand, particularly in the fast-growing computer industry.

Since the early 1970s, US industrial policies generally have been framework policies aimed at providing the appropriate environment for development of the semiconductor and other industries: maintaining macroeconomic conditions conducive to investment; enforcing regulatory and antitrust controls to maintain competition in the industry; supporting educational policies to improve the quality and number of electronic engineers; combatting the unfair trade practices of other countries; and stimulating research through tax incentives and provisions for joint industrial research.

The US Government also supports semiconductor industry research and development through defence and other programmes. In 1986, the government provided an estimated $552 million in research support primarily through the Department of Defense (75 per cent). The VHSIC programme, launched in 1980, has received the greatest funding. Like most other government research programmes, it is oriented towards military objectives and the principal participants are defence contractors. Among the aims of the VHSIC programme are to bring specialised defence semiconductor producers up to pre-existing commercial standards and to improve production technology by developing better process and testing equipment. For national security reasons, VHSIC project participants are forbidden from using VHSIC technologies in commercial applications. More recently, the government modified legal restraints to cooperative research to encourage interaction between industrial, government and university-based programmes. The Semiconductor Research Corporation (SRC) is a consortium of us semiconductor firms which supports university research with some US Government participation; the Microelectronics and Computer Corporation (MCC) is a wider collaboration of the US electronics industry which includes semiconductor producers.

The Semiconductor Manufacturing Technology Institute (SEMATECH), initiated in Spring 1987, is the most recent US industrial policy initiative aimed at improving the competitiveness of the domestic semiconductor industry. Partially funded by the US Department of

Defense ($100 million annually for five years), SEMATECH includes the giants of the US semiconductor industry – including IBM, AT&T and INTEL – in a cooperative research effort to improve manufacturing technologies, equipment and techniques. Goals include the development of production technology for the 64M chip, improvements in manufacturing quality and implementation of flexible manufacturing methods. While spreading risks and costs among companies, SEMATECH hopes to develop competitive technologies for use by all participants and to encourage cooperative standard-setting and other industry synergies. The consortium has so far excluded foreign-owned companies for national security reasons.

Trade initiatives have been an important US Government policy instrument for the semiconductor industry in recent years. The US-Japan Semiconductor Trade Arrangement, signed in September 1986 for a period to mid-1991, is designed to prevent dumping by Japanese firms and to increase Japanese market access to foreign firms. During 1985, the US Government initiated four unfair trade cases involving Japanese semiconductors – a Section 301 case, and antidumping investigations covering 64K DRAMs, EPROMs, and 256K and above DRAMs. After coming to a preliminary affirmative determination, the US Government imposed duties on 64K DRAMs in December 1985. The government imposed a final antidumping order on 64K DRAMs in June 1986. On the basis of antidumping suspension agreements signed between the US Department of Commerce and the Japanese producers, the US Government suspended the antidumping investigations on EPROMs and 256K and above DRAMs in July and August 1986, respectively. The US-Japan Semiconductor Trade Arrangement stemmed from the investigation conducted under Section 301.

In April 1987, the United States imposed 100 per cent tariffs on $300 million of Japanese electronics exports after the alleged failure of Japan to implement fully certain provisions of the Arrangement. The increased duties on imports valued at $135 million were suspended in two stages in June and November 1987 once it appeared that alleged Japanese dumping of semiconductors in third markets had ceased. The remaining sanctions are intended to address the perceived lack of progress in improving foreign access to the Japanese semiconductor market.

B.   Japan

The most significant factor in the early development of the semiconductor industry in Japan was the type and timing of government policies which provided a technology push. Recognising the technology lag with the United States, the Japanese Government fostered, focused and coordinated company activities and research. In addition to maintaining a closed domestic market, Japanese industrial policy for semiconductors was one of setting technological targets and establishing joint research facilities to achieve them. Japanese government support was disbursed with great planning facilitated by continuing dialogue between government and industry. Semiconductor research in Japan has been unique in the large share funded by the private sector, the emphasis on commercial objectives and the extent of joint activity.

In 1975, MITI and NTT, the national telephone company, set up a joint programme with Japanese semiconductor producers to develop VLSI (Very Large Scale Integration) technology which enabled the industry to penetrate the international market with the 64K DRAM. Between 1976 and 1979, the VLSI programme accounted for more than 15 per cent of all semiconductor R&D and was unmatched by programmes in other countries. The support of the government and NTT, which maintained research laboratories and worked closely with companies in developing chip technology, was key to the production of high-density DRAMs where the Japanese mounted their main trade challenge and which they now dominate.

The Japanese Government sponsors many semiconductor research and development projects, including the supercomputer project, the fifth generation computer project, the superlattice project, the quantum effects project, the three-dimensional IC project and the optoelectronics project, in the precompetitive, basic research stages. More recently, a joint industry-government research programme has been initiated on X-ray lithography, considered a crucial chip manufacturing process of the future. The Japanese Government is now encouraging greater attention to basic science and research in part to ease high-technology trade frictions.

Trade policy instruments have been a main Japanese tool for fostering its semiconductor industry; these included quotas and tariffs on semiconductor imports, restrictive controls on foreign investment and official monitoring of licensing agreements. Although Japan protected its home market during the infancy and adolescence of the semiconductor industry, formal controls have been gradually phased out. Semiconductor tariffs were reduced starting in 1972 and eliminated in 1985. Investment restrictions, which were maintained until 1974, were exempted for the American firms IBM and Texas Instruments but these companies had to agree to restrictive licensing arrangements. Japanese licensing terms often required that technologies be made available not only to a single firm but to the whole industry.

Japan is attempting to increase the foreign share of domestic semiconductor sales to reduce trade frictions. In certain end-use markets such as automotive electronics, foreign firms account for only 2 per cent of sales. Japan's trade competitors would like access to at least 20 per cent of the domestic market. It is difficult for foreigners to sell to Japanese electronics producers due to their traditional exclusion, close producer-consumer relationships and the complicated distribution system. In May 1988, Japanese semiconductor purchasers, including Hitachi, NEC and Toshiba, formed a committee within the Electronic Industries Association of Japan to help foreign chip makers gain better access to the Japanese market. MITI also established the International Semiconductor Cooperation Center (INSEC) to assist foreign companies wishing to penetrate the Japanese market.

As part of the US-Japan Semiconductor Trade Arrangement, the government monitored the export prices of certain semiconductor products. However, a GATT panel in mid-1988 found that MITI's method of implementing the third country prevention of dumping provision of the Arrangement formed a "coherent system" which operated as a restriction on exports inconsistent with the GATT. The third country monitoring system has since been amended to bring it into conformity with the GATT.

C. Europe

The European semiconductor industry developed in the absence of either a technology pull or push from government policies. Military and public sector procurement was far less significant than in the United States. Government policies were generally designed to reinforce the existing strategies of firms rather than direct them to new endeavours. The development of the European semiconductor industry was thus slower and more haphazard than in the United States and Japan. The large European companies entered the field at different times and devoted few resources to semiconductors in the 1950s and 1960s. Most firms were involved in consumer electronics (e.g., Philips and Thomson) or heavy electrical engineering (e.g., Siemens and AEG) and tended to neglect advanced component and computer applications where the greatest technical advances were made.

In the period up to the mid-1960s, European Governments did not intervene in semiconductor development apart from some support for defence-related R&D (United Kingdom and France) and procurement preferences for telecommunications and space programmes. In the mid-1960s to mid-1970s, official interest in the development of computers led to some support for semiconductor research. And from the mid-1970s, the larger European countries started to give specific support for semiconductor R&D. However, the European countries tended to follow a pattern of technological imitation with a time lag of up to three to four years in commercial development. European firms acquired US and Japanese technology through licensing, joint ventures and acquisitions but have been less successful at product development. Some governments adopted structural policies for reshaping the semiconductor industry through mergers and goverment ownership, but these were not fully successful due largely to the lack of a science base and scale economies.

The strengthening of the European Community should be a means for improving the competitiveness of the semiconductor industry. It is expected that the planned single market after 1992 will facilitate marketing, public procurement as well as interfirm cooperation. A common infrastructure based on a shared regulatory system, the harmonisation of industry standards, a large, integrated internal market and cooperative research should give a boost to high-technology industries such as semiconductors. The European single market after 1992 has the potential to be advantageous for non-European producers of integrated circuits.

Cooperative European research projects have already upgraded European semiconductor capabilities. In the EC ESPRIT project, leading electronics firms are undertaking basic research on various aspects of information technologies, including VLSI circuits. In its next phase (1990-1994), with total funding of about $1 billion, ESPRIT will include the development of ASICs. The EUREKA project, a non-EC joint research venture with government participation, is also emphasizing basic research on VLSI technology. Both ESPRIT and EUREKA have increased collaboration between small and large semiconductor firms and universities and may be influencing industry structure, as in the merger between France's Thomson and Italy's SGS and the proposed acquisition of Plessey (UK) by Siemens (Germany) and General Electric Co. (UK).

In another research programme, Philips and Siemens are collaborating in the Megaproject to develop large-scale memory chips. The Megaproject is a 5-year joint programme launched in 1985 between Siemens and Philips, with the support of the Governments of Germany and the Netherlands. Plans are now underway to expand this to include SGS-Thomson in a Joint European Submicron Silicon Initiative (JESSI) to run from 1988 to 1995. The aim is to match US and Japanese efforts in developing technologies for the submicron features that will mark high-density memory and logic chips in the 1990s. JESSI will include basic research, development of product technology, circuit applications and a stronger focus on materials and equipment including a pilot production line. About $1 billion of the total investment of $2-$4 billion is to be financed by the participating European governments.

The European Community has maintained relatively high tariffs to protect its semiconductor industry. The EC did not agree to any tariff reductions during the Tokyo Round of the GATT negotiations. However, the EC Common External Tariff of 17.5 per cent on semiconductor imports was lowered in 1986 to 14 per cent. Antidumping investigations were initiated by the European Community in 1987 against Japanese imports of DRAMs, EPROMS and semiconductor wafers. In 1990, the European industry filed a dumping case against Korean producers of DRAMs. In early 1990, the European Community concluded price undertakings with Japanese producers of DRAMs, thus bringing an end to EC investigations into the dumping of Japanese DRAMs on the European market. The European Community also recently revised its rules of origin for semiconductors, defining the "last substantial transformation" as the location of diffusion. The European Community had filed a complaint that the monitoring and market access measures taken under the US-Japan Semiconductor Trade Arrangement violated GATT provisions and were negatively affecting EC consumers of semiconductors. European producers were also concerned that US semiconductor suppliers might be favoured as Japan increased access to its domestic market. However, a GATT Panel determined that the Arrangement provided equal opportunities for all non-Japanese semiconductor companies in Japan.

D. Other OECD

Canada and Australia have small semiconductor industries focused on the local market. Canada has three integrated circuit wafer fabrication lines, Gennum, Mitel and Northern Telecom, and several smaller design and finishing facilities. Australia has two producers of integrated circuits, AWA MicroElectronics and Philips, and two assembly facilities; AWA is now designing and manufacturing ASIC chips. Both countries have trade deficits in semiconductors and rely largely on imports of components for electronic systems production.

Most of the smaller OECD semiconductor producers like Canada and Australia conduct research on semiconductor technology in national facilities and universities and maintain various tax and incentive schemes to encourage microelectronics research in the private sector. However, smaller producers find it difficult to compete in the world semiconductor market which is dominated by the United States and Japan. They are better at developing specialised skills in the design and production of semiconductors which correspond to the needs of local electronics producers. Canada is encouraging investment in its microelectronics industry which is oriented to medium volume production of high value-added products for local producers. Australia is considering increased production for niche markets to build on its custom design skills while allowing economies of scale through more focused output.

E. Non-OECD Countries

Non-OECD semiconductor production is led by Korea and Taiwan whose firms accounted for 3 per cent of world sales in 1988. For many years the site of semiconductor assembly by multinational firms, the Asian NIES are building an indigenous chip industry based on foreign technology, their large domestic electronics markets and their integrated electronics firms. Government support for start-up costs and research as well as trade protection have contributed to growth in semiconductor output. In Korea, investment in facilities increased after the government designated semiconductors a strategic industry in 1983 and provided a $400 million stimulation package. Firms used low-cost capital to branch out from the production of low-end discrete devices and circuits to DRAMS and other VLSIs. Firms have also built on collaborations with OECD firms, such as Hyundai's purchase of technology from Texas Instruments in exchange for a share of output and the Taiwan Semiconductor Manufacturing Company's collaboration with Philips. Several new firms are starting up in Taiwan and Singapore with expected sales of $300 million in 1989 (see Table 57).

Non-OECD governments are reinforcing basic research to develop their own semiconductor technology. The Korean firms Samsung, Hyundai and Goldstar are pooling their research resources at the government's Electronics and Telecommunications Research Institute to

Table 57. **Major Non-OECD Semiconductor Firms: 1988**

Firm		Sales (mil. US$)	Investment (mil. US$)
Korea	Samsung	900	200
	Hyundai	200	100
	Goldstar	120	300
Taiwan	United Microelectronics Corp. (UMC)	130	170
	Taiwan Semiconductor Mfg. Co. (TSMC)	0	220
	Hua Lon	0	70
	Walsin Lihwa	0	70
Singapore	Chartered Semiconductors	0	50

Source: Far Eastern Economic Review, August 1988.

develop a 4M DRAM; research funding is also channeled into the industry by the Korea Institute of Electronics Technology (KIET). In Taiwan, the government's Electronics Research and Service Organisation (ERSO) is working with domestic firms to develop custom design technology. The Singapore Government is sponsoring a joint research and fabrication venture focusing on ASICs for use in telecommunications systems. The recently formed Chartered Semiconductors is a joint venture between the government-owned Singapore Technology Corp. (STC) and the US firms Sierra Semiconductor and National Semiconductor. Other countries such as Hong Kong, Thailand, Malaysia and Brazil are also initiating indigenous production of various semiconductor devices.

Export incentives and import restrictions have been major policy instruments used by the NIEs in the development of their semiconductor industries, although most are now following strategies of trade liberalisation. In 1987, Korea removed restrictions on imports of foreign-produced semiconductors for domestic use and Taiwan has also lowered trade barriers to chip imports. Both countries have given favourable customs treatment to semiconductor equipment imports by indigenous producers. Korea has obtained foreign technology through the strict terms of its licensing and joint venture agreements in contrast to Singapore which has few restrictions on foreign investment. The Asian NIEs have also followed export-oriented strategies where competitiveness is enhanced by exchange rate policies. The limited protection given to intellectual property rights including chip designs has led to increasing frictions with OECD countries.

V. MAJOR POLICY ISSUES

A. Technology and Pricing

One issue raised by recent semiconductor trade disputes is the relationship between technology and pricing. High-technology sectors such as semiconductors are especially conducive to the use of aggressive pricing strategies. Here, economic competition partially depends on relative speed in moving along learning-based cost curves. In semiconductor markets, cost and price levels fall rapidly over the product cycle for each generation of memory chip. Production costs for most semiconductor products decrease by over 30 per cent for every doubling of cumulative volume leading to steep price declines. Firms often price products based on longer-term estimates of average costs, making it difficult to determine the "fairness" of product prices in relation to costs at any given point in time.

This phenomenon has raised questions about the definition of dumping in international trade, where fair value is partly based on the relationship of prices to costs. Under the GATT, antidumping duties may be levied if the price of a product exported from one country to another is less than the home market price, the export price to third countries or the production cost in the home country plus reasonable cost and profit. Both the United States and Europe have used constructed values to determine fair market prices for semiconductor imports in antidumping investigations. Japanese companies were alleged to have sold 64K DRAMs, 256K and above DRAMs and EPROMs in the United States below constructed value causing material injury to the US semiconductor industry.

Japanese firms maintain such calculations may overestimate costs in not taking into account their more advanced position on technology-based learning curves in the production of semiconductors and their longer-term views of pricing. They have also contested other aspects of the calculation of constructed values and dumping margins in antidumping investigations. In view of recent trade tensions, the definition of dumping and the calculation of fair market prices may need to be reviewed for high-technology sectors such as semiconductors. Traditional definitions of dumping may be too static for sectors where competition is based on the ability to participate in markets with short product cycles and learning-based cost curves. Many dumping investigations may be based on timeframes which do not take into account the interaction of costs and prices over the life of the chip. Some believe current dumping regulations are unable to deal fairly with high-technology products whose prices reflect obsolescence measured in months. However, for products such as semiconductors, it is often difficult to distinguish cost-based pricing from unfair pricing and marketing methods aimed at achieving dominant positions in world markets.

B. New Types of Trade Measures

The US-Japan Semiconductor Trade Agreement, signed in 1986, and the recently concluded EC-Japan price undertakings are examples of a new type of bilateral trade measure whose status under the GATT is not clear and which are called grey-area measures. Governments may prefer grey-area arrangements because the scope and speed of action is greater than that achieved through multilateral safeguard procedures which are subject to strict criteria, or because safeguard procedures would not provide an appropriate or effective mechanism for addressing the trade problems in question. Such measures may be used to obtain trade objectives such as the opening of foreign markets or increased protection of intellectual property rights. A main objective of the US-Japan Semiconductor Trade Arrangement is to widen access to Japan's semiconductor market, while the EC-Japan price undertaking is intended to prevent dumping. Whatever their purpose, grey-area measures may represent bilateralism rather than multilateralism in international trade.

There are proposals to make grey-area measures more transparent and subject to international trade rules. Some believe that new GATT provisions are needed to make government use of these measures subject to procedures and criteria just as strict as those used for other instruments of trade protection. Others propose specific rules prohibiting governments from entering into arrangements which may lead to managed trade. A concurrent approach is to resolve trade problems such as those in the semiconductor industry through more informal industry channels. It is recommended that governments do a full assessment of the costs and benefits of such trade measures due to their often negative effects on consumers, their sometimes questionable benefits for the industries concerned and their often unforeseen side effects.

C. Industrial Policies for High-Technology Industries

Most government policies for the semiconductor industry are based on the view that an indigenous semiconductor industry is essential to economic growth and national security. Semiconductors are central to the development of information-age technology which is the driving force in the OECD economies. The contribution of semiconductors to the cost of downstream electronics systems is generally small – usually well below ten per cent of total systems costs – but the performance contributions are immeasurable. Semiconductors often embody functions specific to a particular end-use, which increases the importance of close producer-user relationships and the integrated production of semiconductors and electronics systems. For these reasons, countries which produce consumer electronics and other electronics products may desire a domestic source of integrated circuits. The strategic implications of semiconductors for competitiveness in other electronics products has led governments to use both industrial and trade policies to protect and nourish the industry in its infant stage as well as in its maturity.

National security concerns are another policy consideration because of the importance of semiconductors to defence electronics. Sectors which develop dual-use technologies with both military and commercial applications could be negatively affected by a deterioration of an indigenous semiconductor industry and its suppliers. Countries are fearful of depending on foreign-produced integrated circuits which they may find unavailable in time of war or international crisis. These concerns have led countries to place limits on foreign ownership of semiconductor facilities and to adopt other trade and investment policies aimed at maintaining a domestic semiconductor manufacturing base.

Most of these fears center on the production of one type of semiconductor – DRAMs. The production of DRAMs is believed to be a "technology driver" in leading and stimulating technological progress throughout the semiconductor industry. It is thought that the experience gained through producing DRAMs cannot be achieved through lower volume commodity products or custom devices. The learning curve advantages derived from DRAM production cannot be transferred through licensing or foreign investment. Countries fear that if they lose or do not develop the capacity to produce DRAMs, they will be eliminated from the race to produce future generations of DRAMs as well as other types of semiconductors.

While some countries need to maintain a semiconductor production base which includes the capability to produce memories for defence and economic reasons, this need may be declining somewhat in other countries due to the internationalisation of production and marketing and changing product demand. The product profile of the industry is changing with custom and semi-custom circuits in growing demand. Scale economies and technology driver effects may be attainable in some countries through production of certain industry-specific chips. Despite occasional shortages, most semiconductor products are readily available on a highly competitive international market. Semiconductor producers are willing to work closely with end-users to customise their chips for specific systems. Extensive foreign investment has led to production of semiconductors in most OECD countries.

OECD governments use a combination of industrial policy instruments (mostly research subsidies) and trade policy instruments (mostly import controls) in support of their semiconductor industries. Studies show that traditional industrial policy instruments such as R&D support are more likely than trade measures to stimulate the development of high-technology sectors. However, there is concern that semiconductor research is becoming increasingly centralised in a few OECD countries and firms. Proposals have been made for more joint research and development programmes on semiconductor technology among the OECD countries. There may also be a need for new guidelines regarding reciprocal international access to government-sponsored research on semiconductor technology.

While current industrial policies for semiconductors do not appear to be distorting trade flows, trade policies may be impeding the ability of the industry to respond to current demand and technology trends. In general, it is likely that trade frictions in semiconductors will continue in the absence of a wider market opening in Japan and decreased use of protectionist measures in other OECD countries. The use of trade policy instruments needs to be made more transparent, to take account of effects on consumers and to have built-in mechanisms for assessment and termination. Trade measures should also be used in conjunction with industrial policy measures which facilitate restructuring or movement to a higher technology level. The challenge to OECD policymakers is to use a combination of industrial and trade policy instruments which promote competitiveness rather than inefficiency and which are in step with current semiconductor industry trends.

REFERENCES

Benn Electronics Publications (1987), *1988 Yearbook of Electronics Data,* United Kingdom.

Canadian Department for Regional Industrial Expansion (1988), "Information Package to Assist Investment in Microelectronics in Canada", August.

Commissariat Général du Plan (1986), "L'électronique: un défi planétaire, un enjeu: l'Europe", Paris, December.

Dosi, G. (1983), "Semiconductors: Europe's Precarious Survival in High Technology," in Geoffrey Shepherd *et al.* (eds.), *Europe's Industries: Public and Private Strategies for Change,* , London, Frances Pinter.

Finan, W.F. and Amundsen, C.B. (1986), "Modeling U.S.-Japan Competition in Semiconductors", *Journal of Policy Modeling,* 8:3.

Malerba, F. (1985), "Demand Structure and Technological Change: The Case of the European Semiconductor Industry", *Research Policy,* No. 14.

Mody, A. and Wheeler, D. (1987), "Prices, Costs and Competition at the Technology Frontier: A Model for Semiconductor Memories", *Journal of Policy Modeling,* 9:2.

OECD (1985), *The Semiconductor Industry: Trade-Related Issues,* Paris.

"The Report into the Australian Electronic Components Industry" (1987), prepared by BIS Shrapnel for the Communications Equipment Industry Strategy Coordinating Committee, November.

United Nations Centre on Transnational Corporations (1986), "Transnational Corporations in the International Semiconductor Industry", New York, United Nations.

US Federal Interagency Staff Working Group (1987), *The Semiconductor Industry,* November.

MAIN SALES OUTLETS OF OECD PUBLICATIONS – PRINCIPAUX POINTS DE VENTE DES PUBLICATIONS DE L'OCDE

Argentina – Argentine
Carlos Hirsch S.R.L.
Galería Güemes, Florida 165, 4° Piso
1333 Buenos Aires — Tel. (1) 331.1787 y 331.2391
Telefax: (1) 331.1787

Australia – Australie
D.A. Book (Aust.) Pty. Ltd.
648 Whitehorse Road, P.O.B 163
Mitcham, Victoria 3132 — Tel. (03) 873.4411
Telefax: (03) 873.5679

Austria – Autriche
OECD Publications and Information Centre
Schedestrasse 7
D-W 5300 Bonn 1 (Germany) — Tel. (49.228) 21.60.45
Telefax: (49.228) 26.11.04

Gerold & Co.
Graben 31
Wien I — Tel. (0222) 533.50.14

Belgium – Belgique
Jean De Lannoy
Avenue du Roi 202
B-1060 Bruxelles — Tel. (02) 538.51.69/538.08.41
Telefax: (02) 538.08.41

Canada
Renouf Publishing Company Ltd.
1294 Algoma Road
Ottawa, ON K1B 3W8 — Tel. (613) 741.4333
Telefax: (613) 741.5439

Stores:
61 Sparks Street
Ottawa, ON K1P 5R1 — Tel. (613) 238.8985
211 Yonge Street
Toronto, ON M5B 1M4 — Tel. (416) 363.3171

Federal Publications
165 University Avenue
Toronto, ON M5H 3B8 — Tel. (416) 581.1552
Telefax: (416)581.1743

Les Éditions La Liberté Inc.
3020 Chemin Sainte-Foy
Sainte-Foy, PQ G1X 3V6 — Tel. (418) 658.3763
Telefax: (418) 658.3763

China – Chine
China National Publications Import
Export Corporation (CNPIEC)
P.O. Box 88
Beijing — Tel. 44.0731
Telefax: 401.5661

Denmark – Danemark
Munksgaard Export and Subscription Service
35, Nørre Søgade, P.O. Box 2148
DK-1016 København K — Tel. (33) 12.85.70
Telefax: (33) 12.93.87

Finland – Finlande
Akateeminen Kirjakauppa
Keskuskatu 1, P.O. Box 128
00100 Helsinki — Tel. (358 0) 12141
Telefax: (358 0) 121.4441

France
OECD/OCDE
Mail Orders/Commandes par correspondance:
2, rue André-Pascal
75775 Paris Cédex 16 — Tel. (33-1) 45.24.82.00
Telefax: (33-1) 45.24.85.00
or (33-1) 45.24.81.76
Telex: 620 160 OCDE

Bookshop/Librairie:
33, rue Octave-Feuillet
75016 Paris — Tel. (33-1) 45.24.81.67
(33-1) 45.24.81.81

Librairie de l'Université
12a, rue Nazareth
13100 Aix-en-Provence — Tel. 42.26.18.08
Telefax: 42.26.63.26

Germany – Allemagne
OECD Publications and Information Centre
Schedestrasse 7
D-W 5300 Bonn 1 — Tel. (0228) 21.60.45
Telefax: (0228) 26.11.04

Greece – Grèce
Librairie Kauffmann
Mavrokordatou 9
106 78 Athens — Tel. 322.21.60
Telefax: 363.39.67

Hong Kong
Swindon Book Co. Ltd.
13 - 15 Lock Road
Kowloon, Hong Kong — Tel. 366.80.31
Telefax: 739.49.75

Iceland – Islande
Mál Mog Menning
Laugavegi 18, Pósthólf 392
121 Reykjavik — Tel. 162.35.23

India – Inde
Oxford Book and Stationery Co.
Scindia House
New Delhi 110001 — Tel.(11) 331.5896/5308
Telefax: (11) 332.5993

17 Park Street
Calcutta 700016 — Tel. 240832

Indonesia – Indonésie
Pdii-Lipi
P.O. Box 269/JKSMG/88
Jakarta 12790 — Tel. 583467
Telex: 62 875

Ireland – Irlande
TDC Publishers – Library Suppliers
12 North Frederick Street
Dublin 1 — Tel. 74.48.35/74.96.77
Telefax: 74.84.16

Israel
Electronic Publications only
Publications électroniques seulement
Sophist Systems Ltd.
71 Allenby Street
Tel-Aviv 65134 — Tel. 3-29.00.21
Telefax: 3-29.92.39

Italy – Italie
Libreria Commissionaria Sansoni
Via Duca di Calabria 1/1
50125 Firenze — Tel. (055) 64.54.15
Telefax: (055) 64.12.57

Via Bartolini 29
20155 Milano — Tel. (02) 36.50.83
Editrice e Libreria Herder
Piazza Montecitorio 120
00186 Roma — Tel. 679.46.28
Telex: NATEL I 621427

Libreria Hoepli
Via Hoepli 5
20121 Milano — Tel. (02) 86.54.46
Telefax: (02) 805.28.86

Libreria Scientifica
Dott. Lucio de Biasio 'Aeiou'
Via Meravigli 16
20123 Milano — Tel. (02) 805.68.98
Telefax: (02) 80.01.75

Japan – Japon
OECD Publications and Information Centre
Landic Akasaka Building
2-3-4 Akasaka, Minato-ku
Tokyo 107 — Tel. (81.3) 3586.2016
Telefax: (81.3) 3584.7929

Korea – Corée
Kyobo Book Centre Co. Ltd.
P.O. Box 1658, Kwang Hwa Moon
Seoul — Tel. 730.78.91
Telefax: 735.00.30

Malaysia – Malaisie
Co-operative Bookshop Ltd.
University of Malaya
P.O. Box 1127, Jalan Pantai Baru
59700 Kuala Lumpur
Malaysia — Tel. 756.5000/756.5425
Telefax: 757.3661

Netherlands – Pays-Bas
SDU Uitgeverij
Christoffel Plantijnstraat 2
Postbus 20014
2500 EA's-Gravenhage — Tel. (070 3) 78.99.11
Voor bestellingen: — Tel. (070 3) 78.98.80
Telefax: (070 3) 47.63.51

New Zealand – Nouvelle-Zélande
GP Publications Ltd.
Customer Services
33 The Esplanade - P.O. Box 38-900
Petone, Wellington — Tel. (04) 5685.555
Telefax: (04) 5685.333

Norway – Norvège
Narvesen Info Center - NIC
Bertrand Narvesens vei 2
P.O. Box 6125 Etterstad
0602 Oslo 6 — Tel. (02) 57.33.00
Telefax: (02) 68.19.01

Pakistan
Mirza Book Agency
65 Shahrah Quaid-E-Azam
Lahore 3 — Tel. 66.839
Telex: 44886 UBL PK. Attn: MIRZA BK

Portugal
Livraria Portugal
Rua do Carmo 70-74
Apart. 2681
1117 Lisboa Codex — Tel.: (01) 347.49.82/3/4/5
Telefax: (01) 347.02.64

Singapore – Singapour
Information Publications Pte. Ltd.
Pei-Fu Industrial Building
24 New Industrial Road No. 02-06
Singapore 1953 — Tel. 283.1786/283.1798
Telefax: 284.8875

Spain – Espagne
Mundi-Prensa Libros S.A.
Castelló 37, Apartado 1223
Madrid 28001 — Tel. (91) 431.33.99
Telefax: (91) 575.39.98

Libreria Internacional AEDOS
Consejo de Ciento 391
08009 - Barcelona — Tel. (93) 488.34.92
Telefax: (93) 487.76.59

Llibreria de la Generalitat
Palau Moja
Rambla dels Estudis, 118
08002 - Barcelona — Tel. (93) 318.80.12 (Subscripcions)
(93) 302.67.23 (Publicacions)
Telefax: (93) 412.18.54

Sri Lanka
Centre for Policy Research
c/o Colombo Agencies Ltd.
No. 300-304, Galle Road
Colombo 3 — Tel. (1) 574240, 573551-2
Telefax: (1) 575394, 510711

Sweden – Suède
Fritzes Fackboksföretaget
Box 16356
Regeringsgatan 12
103 27 Stockholm — Tel. (08) 23.89.00
Telefax: (08) 20.50.21

Subscription Agency/Abonnements:
Wennergren-Williams AB
Nordenflychtsvägen 74
Box 30004
104 25 Stockholm — Tel. (08) 13.67.00
Telefax: (08) 618.62.32

Switzerland – Suisse
OECD Publications and Information Centre
Schedestrasse 7
D-W 5300 Bonn 1 (Germany) — Tel. (49.228) 21.60.45
Telefax: (49.228) 26.11.04

Suisse romande
Maditec S.A.
Chemin des Palettes 4
1020 Renens/Lausanne — Tel. (021) 635.08.65
Telefax: (021) 635.07.80

Librairie Payot
6 rue Grenus
1211 Genève 11 — Tel. (022) 731.89.50
Telex: 28356

Subscription Agency – Service des Abonnements
Naville S.A.
7, rue Lévrier
1201 Genève — Tél.: (022) 732.24.00
Telefax: (022) 738.87.13

Taiwan – Formose
Good Faith Worldwide Int'l. Co. Ltd.
9th Floor, No. 118, Sec. 2
Chung Hsiao E. Road
Taipei — Tel. (02) 391.7396/391.7397
Telefax: (02) 394.9176

Thailand – Thaïlande
Suksit Siam Co. Ltd.
113, 115 Fuang Nakhon Rd.
Opp. Wat Rajbopith
Bangkok 10200 — Tel. (662) 251.1630
Telefax: (662) 236.7783

Turkey – Turquie
Kültur Yayinlari Is-Türk Ltd. Sti.
Atatürk Bulvari No. 191/Kat. 21
Kavaklidere/Ankara — Tel. 25.07.60
Dolmabahce Cad. No. 29
Besiktas/Istanbul — Tel. 160.71.88
Telex: 43482B

United Kingdom – Royaume-Uni
HMSO
Gen. enquiries — Tel. (071) 873 0011
Postal orders only:
P.O. Box 276, London SW8 5DT
Personal Callers HMSO Bookshop
49 High Holborn, London WC1V 6HB
Telefax: 071 873 2000
Branches at: Belfast, Birmingham, Bristol, Edinburgh,
Manchester

United States – États-Unis
OECD Publications and Information Centre
2001 L Street N.W., Suite 700
Washington, D.C. 20036-4910 — Tel. (202) 785.6323
Telefax: (202) 785.0350

Venezuela
Libreria del Este
Avda F. Miranda 52, Aptdo. 60337
Edificio Galipán
Caracas 106 — Tel. 951.1705/951.2307/951.1297
Telegram: Libreste Caracas

Yugoslavia – Yougoslavie
Jugoslovenska Knjiga
Knez Mihajlova 2, P.O. Box 36
Beograd — Tel. (011) 621.992
Telefax: (011) 625.970

Orders and inquiries from countries where Distributors have
not yet been appointed should be sent to: OECD Publications Service, 2 rue André-Pascal, 75775 Paris Cédex 16,
France.

Les commandes provenant de pays où l'OCDE n'a pas
encore désigné de distributeur devraient être adressées à :
OCDE, Service des Publications, 2, rue André-Pascal, 75775
Paris Cédex 16, France.

OECD PUBLICATIONS, 2 rue André-Pascal, 75775 PARIS CEDEX 16
PRINTED IN FRANCE
(70 92 01 1) ISBN 92-64-13627-4 - No. 45867 1992